BELOVED

This is YOUR year to create.
Make it an AMAZING year,
using your intuition and your
Tarot cards as a guide.

BIDDY TAROT

ACKNOWLEDGEMENTS

A big, heart-felt thank you to Tassia Assis for designing the layout of the Biddy Tarot Planner; Jen Martin for co-creating the New and Full Moon spreads and proofreading the Planner; Laura Hatajik for sharing the Crystal of the Month; Team Biddy for bringing the Planner to life; and the Biddy Tarot community for your ongoing love and support.

The Tarot deck featured in the 2020 Biddy Tarot Planner is the Lumina Tarot, republished with permission from the author, Lauren Aletta from Inner Hue. The Lumina Tarot is available for sale via **www.biddytarot.com/lumina.**

Note: The exact date of lunations may vary depending on your region. This planner was made using PDT Timezone (UTC -7; Los Angeles, Vancouver). To know the exact dates for your region, go to www.timeanddate.com/moon/phases.

WELCOME

Welcome, Beloved, to 2020: The Year of Aligned Action.

You are about to step into one of your most powerful years yet as you say YES to your intuition and your inner wisdom. With your Tarot cards as a guide, you'll tune in to your Higher Self, manifest your goals and dreams and most importantly, create a life that is in full alignment with your soul's purpose.

It's all possible with the Biddy Tarot Planner.

The Biddy Tarot Planner will give you the power to:

- ⊙ Tap into the collective energy of each month with the intuitive Tarot forecast

- ⊙ Use monthly rituals to deepen your connection with the collective energy

- ⊙ Explore the blessings of each new and full moon

- ⊙ Create personalized daily forecasts to maximize the potential of each day

- ⊙ Complete juicy Tarot spreads for each season and connect with what the upcoming year has in store for you

This Planner has been designed for YOU, to help you create an amazing year ahead, with your intuition and Tarot cards as a guide. So, get out your favorite Tarot deck, crystals, and markers and prepare to get 'up close and personal' with your intuition and inner wisdom.

Lots of love and success,

[signature]

P.S.

We love celebrating our community (and that means you!) So, don't forget to share LOTS of photos and videos of your Planner on Instagram, using the hashtag **#biddytarotplanner**. And make sure you're following **@biddytarot** as we'll be sharing lots more tips to help you create more aligned action this year, using Tarot as your guide.

FREE BONUS:
BIDDY TAROT PLANNER KIT

To help you get the most out of your 2020 Biddy Tarot Planner, I've created a free bonus kit, including:

⊙ Video tutorials on how to use the Planner

⊙ Full Moon & New Moon Rituals and Visualizations to maximize the power and potency of the lunar cycles

⊙ A guide to navigating Mercury Retrograde and a special Mercury Retrograde Tarot spread

⊙ Print-your-own Tarot cards to use inside of the Planner

⊙ Access to November & December from the 2019 Biddy Tarot Planner so you can get started straight away

⊙ And so much more!

Download the free Planner Kit at
www.biddytarot.com/planner-bonus

TABLE OF CONTENTS

HOW TO MAKE THE MOST OUT OF YOUR PLANNER

To get started, here's what you will need:

- ⊙ Your favorite Tarot deck
- ⊙ Your favorite markers, pens & pencils
- ⊙ Your free Bonus Planner Kit (download the Kit at www.biddytarot.com/planner-bonus/)
- ⊙ (Optional) Tarot stickers (check out https://www.etsy.com/au/market/tarot_card_stickers)

> If you're on Instagram, I would love to see your Tarot spreads! Use the hashtag **#biddytarotplanner** to post your photos of the Planner and your readings, and we'll share them with the Biddy Tarot community!

Here's how you can make the most out of your Planner:

FIRST, WATCH THE VIDEO TUTORIALS...

I've created a series of tutorial videos to show you how to make the most of the Biddy Tarot Planner. I'll be there with you every step of the way!

For free access, go to www.biddytarot.com/planner-bonus.

AT THE START OF THE YEAR...

Start your year with the **New Year Ritual** (on page 16) — a divine experience of self-reflection, intuitive journaling, and Tarot card consultation.

And connect with the energy of the **2020 Tarot card — the Emperor**. Take some time to reflect on what its energy means for you as you step into the new year.

FOR EACH SEASON...

At the start of each season, you'll be invited to do a **Seasonal Tarot Spread** to explore the energy of the season and use that energy to set your goals and intentions for the upcoming three months.

A note on location: The seasons in this Planner have been designed for those in the Northern Hemisphere. If you are in the Southern Hemisphere, please swap the seasons so you're doing the Summer Solstice Tarot Spread in December, and so on.

AT THE START OF THE MONTH...

Reflect on the **Tarot card for the month.** I've shared some initial insights — take it to the next level by connecting in with what it means for you. How can you harness this energy and use it throughout the month ahead?

Next, do the **ritual** associated with the Tarot card. You may do the ritual just once during the month, or you may choose to do it more frequently. You can also continue to use the ritual in following months if you feel called to do so.

I've also recommended a **crystal** that you can work with to connect with the energy of the Tarot card. You could carry the crystal with you throughout the month, wear it, place it on your desk or in your bedroom, bring it out each time you do a Tarot reading — be creative!

Finally, I've noted the **major astrological influences** that are at play during the month so your cards and stars align.

And while we're speaking about planetary influences , keep an eye out for **Mercury Retrograde** which occurs 3 times this year. Mercury Retrograde is renowned for creating havoc with communication, timing, travel and technology. Avoid activities such as signing contracts, launching products, and making technical upgrades, and always double-check the details. That said, there are also positive aspects to Mercury Retrograde — it's the perfect time for reflection, revisiting the past, reworking or closing out a project, and re-evaluating your priorities (lots of 'RE's!!).

For each Mercury Retrograde of the year, you can complete the Mercury Retrograde Tarot Spread to gain clarity through this potentially confusing time. Check out www.biddytarot.com/planner-bonus for the Mercury Retrograde spread.

FOR EACH DAY...

At the beginning of each day, draw a Tarot card and set your intention for the day ahead, noting it in your Planner. At the end of the day, reflect on what you have learned and discovered based on the energy of your daily card.

For more ideas on how to do the daily Tarot card draw, check out www.biddytarot.com/daily-tarot-card/.

ON THE NEW MOON & THE FULL MOON...

Without question, the cycles of the moon have an impact on our own personal cycles. For each New and Full Moon, do the spread that corresponds to the astrological sign of the moon. On the **New Moon,** set your intentions for the next two weeks and get ready to start new projects and make new beginnings. On the **Full Moon,** give thanks for what you have achieved and manifested over the past two weeks, and let go what is no longer serving you, clearing and cleansing your energy and your space. I've created a special New Moon and Full Moon Ritual *plus* two guided visualizations so you can fully tap into the power of the lunar cycles. Access this bonus at www.biddytarot.com/planner-bonus.

Note: All times and dates of the lunar cycles are in US Pacific time.

IF YOU NEED A LITTLE HELP WITH THE TAROT CARD MEANINGS...

To make the most out of the Biddy Tarot Planner, all you need is a basic knowledge of the Tarot cards and your intuition will take care of the rest! However, I know that some of you may want a little extra guidance along the way so I have two options for you:

BOOK - THE ULTIMATE GUIDE TO TAROT CARD MEANINGS

This is my best-selling book with all of the meanings for the Tarot cards inside. Not only will you discover what the upright and reversed cards mean, you'll also learn how they translate in relationship, work, finance, spiritual, and well-being readings.

The best part? These aren't airy-fairy explanations of the cards — these are modern, practical and relatable so that you can quickly decipher the meaning of your Tarot readings. Buy the book at www.biddytarot.com/guide.

ONLINE COURSE - MASTER THE TAROT CARD MEANINGS

 MASTER THE TAROT CARD MEANINGS

My program, Master the Tarot Card Meanings, is the #1 Tarot training online to help you instantly (and intuitively) interpret the 78 cards in the Tarot deck — without memorization.

In Master the Tarot Card Meanings, I'll show you how to build a unique personal connection with the Tarot, using simple yet powerful techniques for interpreting the cards.

I'll teach you the 'must know' systems that sit behind the Tarot cards that make learning Tarot super simple. And together, we'll walk through the 78 Tarot cards, so you can master each and every one of them, once and for all!

Learn more at www.biddytarot.com/mtcm or start with our free training at www.biddytarot.com/webinar-mtcm.

REMEMBER...

- ◎ To make the most out of this Planner, check out my free video tutorials and bonuses at www.biddytarot.com/planner-bonus.

- ◎ Post your photos of your Planner and Tarot spreads to Instagram with the hashtag #biddytarotplanner and we'll give you a shout-out!

WANT TO GET STARTED EARLY?

- ◎ Download the Planner pages for November and December 2019 (for free!) at www.biddytarot.com/planner-bonus so that you can get started straight away.

2019 REFLECTION

As we come to the end of 2019, take some time to reflect on the past 12 months and prepare yourself for the year to come.

For each question, journal your intuitive thoughts first, then if you feel called to do so, draw a Tarot card to help you go deeper.

1. What were my biggest achievements for 2019?

2. What were my biggest challenges for 2019?

3. How have I developed as a person?

4. What did I learn in 2019?

5. How would I describe 2019 in just 3 words?

6. What aspects of 2019 can I leave behind?

7. What aspects of 2019 can I bring with me into 2020?

8. What new seeds and opportunities are being planted?

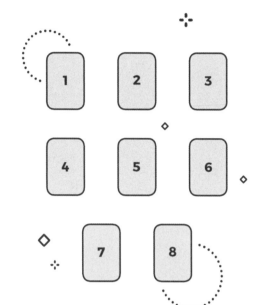

1. WHAT WERE MY BIGGEST ACHIEVEMENTS FOR 2019?

2. WHAT WERE MY BIGGEST CHALLENGES FOR 2019?

3. HOW HAVE I DEVELOPED AS A PERSON?

4. WHAT DID I LEARN IN 2019?

5. HOW WOULD I DESCRIBE 2019 IN JUST 3 WORDS?

6. WHAT ASPECTS OF 2019 CAN I LEAVE BEHIND?

7. WHAT ASPECTS OF 2019 CAN I BRING WITH ME INTO 2020?

8. WHAT NEW SEEDS AND OPPORTUNITIES ARE BEING PLANTED?

2020

2020 TAROT CARD
THE EMPEROR

In 2020—the year of the Emperor—you are being called to build a solid foundation to support your future growth. Success is imminent, so long as you have the right structures in place and the self-discipline to follow through. This is the time for you to tap into the vast power of the Divine masculine and take aligned action to move forward with your goals and ambitions.

Success is coming to you—oh, yes it is! But, in order for you to be able to receive that success and hold it in your energy field in a way that is sustainable, you must first create a solid foundation and structure that can fully support this new level of success.

For example, you can attract great wealth, but if you do not have a way to invest your money or manage your finances, that wealth will disappear as quickly as it arrived (this is also why so many lottery winners end up going broke—because they are not ready to fully receive the sudden flow of cash.)

This year, it is essential that you upgrade your systems and structures—whether in your relationships, career, finances or personal life—to prepare you for the immense opportunity and potential that is coming your way. You need to be ready to hold more, have more, be more. You need to be ready to receive and have the capacity within you to retain what comes into your vortex of energy. Because if you don't upgrade your systems and structures, or if you try to build on a shaky foundation, your success will not last.

In this Emperor year, you are also being called to tap into the power of the Divine masculine and activate your 'yang' energy. This is the year to make things happen, to take action that is aligned with your goals and to move forward with confidence and ambition. You have a huge

2 + 0 + 2 + 0 = 4 – EMPEROR

At its core, the energy of the Emperor is represented by:

- ⊙ Establishing a solid foundation
- ⊙ Taking action and moving forward
- ⊙ Being disciplined and following a structure
- ⊙ Connecting with the Divine masculine energy

opportunity to manifest your dreams and desires, so long as you step up and lead the way. Create calm out of chaos by breaking down any problem into its parts and then mapping out the actions you need to take to resolve it.

Be systematic, strategic and highly organized in your approach, and stick to your plan until the end.

No more waiting around for something to change. Take charge of your life and make it happen!

RITUAL: ALIGNED ACTION

It's action planning time! First, pull the Emperor card from your deck and tune in to his masculine energy. Then, write down your goals for the year. What needs to happen for you to manifest these goals? What will guarantee success? Now, on a new piece of paper, draw four quadrants – one for each quarter of the year. Write in the actions you'll take in each quarter. You may need to move things around so you're not overloaded. Then ask yourself, "What structure do I need in place to commit to these actions and manifest my goals?"

 ## JOURNALING PROMPTS

Use these journaling prompts throughout the year to help you stay in alignment with the Emperor energy.

⊙ What foundations do I need to support my growth and success?

⊙ What actions do I need to take to achieve my goals?

⊙ What does the Divine masculine look like for me?

⊙ How can I apply structure and discipline to my life for greater success?

INSIGHTS

NEW YEAR'S RITUAL

This New Year's Ritual is a beautiful, empowering way to start the new year! You'll be connecting with your Higher Self and envisioning what you truly want to manifest in the year to come. This is about positive change and transformation at a deep, symbolic level that will help you to create an abundant, super-charged year ahead!

I encourage you to use this ritual as a guide only. Rituals become even more powerful when you create them, so use this as a starting point and then get creative with what you want to include.

Ready? Let's do it!

STEP 1: CREATE THE SACRED SPACE

Get everything you need for the ritual, then create your sacred space.

Set up your altar. Now, this doesn't have to be super fancy. Simply place the items you collected that represent what you want to create in 2020. Add in crystals, Tarot cards, jewelry, flowers, rocks—whatever helps you to create a sacred intention for your ritual.

Place the candles in and around your altar. And when you are ready, switch off the lights and light the candles.

Take a moment to ground yourself. Close your eyes and take in a few deep breaths. Connect in with the Earth energy and the Universal energy, feeling yourself filled with a beautiful white light.

STEP 2: REFLECT ON THE PAST YEAR

Reflect on the year that was 2019. What did you experience? What were the highs? What were the lows? And what did you learn along the way? Write down your insights on the next page.

YOU WILL NEED...

⊙ Your Biddy Tarot Planner

⊙ Your favorite Tarot deck – the Everyday Tarot Deck is a great place to start (available via www.everydaytarot.com/deck)

⊙ Your favorite markers

⊙ At least one candle and some matches

⊙ A herbal bundle for clearing and cleansing

⊙ Items for your altar. These are symbols of what you want to create in 2020, such as an image of your ideal relationship, a flower for beauty, a seed pod for starting something new – you choose!

⊙ At least one hour of uninterrupted time. Lock the door, turn off your phone, do whatever you need to protect your sacred space

⊙ (Optional) Your favorite crystals – I recommend citrine for abundance and clear quartz for clarity

⊙ The New Year Spread (Page 20)

INSIGHTS

Take the herbal bundle and light it. Then, wave the smoke around your body, front and back, as you cleanse your aura and release any old energy that may be clinging to you. For each item on your list, say aloud, "I release myself of... {insert what you want to release}."

When you feel complete, say aloud three times, "I give thanks for the past year. I release what no longer serves me. And I welcome new opportunities with open arms."

STEP 3: VISUALIZE WHAT YOU WANT TO CREATE IN 2020

Now, close your eyes and start to imagine what you want to create in 2020.

Think about what you want to create in your relationships. Imagine it as if it were a movie in your mind, experiencing everything you want to experience in your relationships for 2020. See yourself in the movie, being an active participant. See what you see. Hear what you hear. Feel what you feel. Taste what you taste. And smell what you smell. Create a full sensory experience.

When you're ready, wipe the movie screen clean, and bring up a new movie, this time about your career, work and finances. What do you want to create in your material world? Create a full sensory experience.

When you're complete, bring up the next movie for your health and well-being. And after that, your personal development. What do you want to create?

When you feel complete, open your eyes, and write down your experiences on the next page.

Next, take out your Tarot cards and continue with Cards 3 to 9 of the New Year Tarot Spread. Write your cards and insights in the space provided on Page 21.

RELATIONSHIPS

HEALTH & WELL-BEING

CAREER & FINANCES

PERSONAL DEVELOPMENT

STEP 4: MANIFEST YOUR GOALS FOR 2020

Read over your insights from Step 3 and choose 10 things you want to manifest in 2020 (e.g. I want to be fit and healthy, or I want to take a 3-month vacation).

Then, change these to "I am" statements (yes, even if they sound a little funny). For example, "I AM fit and healthy" or "I AM enjoying a 3-month vacation".

Take a moment to feel the energy and the vibration of these "I am" statements – super powerful, right?!

Now, complete your New Year Tarot Spread, from Cards 10 to 12 and write your cards and insights in the space provided on Pages 23 and 24.

And finally, close your eyes and visualize the energy of what you want to create as a bright white light. Imagine it as a ball of light radiating within your solar plexus (just above your belly button). Then imagine the ball of light getting bigger and bigger, filling your body, flowing through your aura, and radiating out into the world. This is your power, your determination, your ability to manifest your goals, just as you see them. And so it is done. When you are ready, gently open your eyes.

STEP 5: CLOSE THE SPACE

Before you close the space, check in with your Higher Self and ask if there is anything else that needs to be done before this ritual is complete. Sometimes your intuition may guide you towards another sacred activity before you know for sure that you are done.

When you're ready, say a prayer of thanks to your Higher Self for guiding you along this process. Then, say out loud, "And so it is."

Blow out the candles, turn on the lights, then pack up the space. You may wish to leave part of your altar there or move it somewhere more convenient, so you have a visual reminder of this beautiful ritual that you have gifted yourself.

INSIGHTS

REMEMBER...

If you need extra guidance for the New Year's Ritual, make sure you watch my free video tutorials at **www.biddytarot.com/planner-bonus**

NEW YEAR SPREAD

Make the most of the new year with the New Year's Tarot Spread. This is a powerful spread to use at the start of the year. Or, use it on your birthday to gain valuable insight into what you might experience during your next year of life.

1. The previous year in summary

2. Lessons learned from the past year

3. Aspirations for the next 12 months

4. What empowers you in reaching your aspirations

5. What may stand in the way of reaching your aspirations

6. Your relationships and emotions in the coming year

7. Your career, work and finances

8. Your health and well-being

9. Your spiritual energy and inner fulfilment

10. What you most need to focus on in the year ahead

11. Your most important lesson for the coming year

12. Overall, where are you headed in the next 12 months

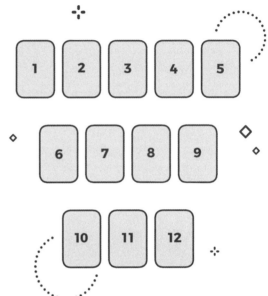

1. THE PREVIOUS YEAR IN SUMMARY

2. LESSONS LEARNED FROM THE PAST YEAR

3. ASPIRATIONS FOR THE NEXT 12 MONTHS

4. WHAT EMPOWERS YOU IN REACHING YOUR ASPIRATIONS

5. WHAT MAY STAND IN THE WAY OF REACHING YOUR ASPIRATIONS

6. YOUR RELATIONSHIPS AND EMOTIONS IN THE COMING YEAR

7. YOUR CAREER, WORK AND FINANCES

8. YOUR HEALTH AND WELL-BEING

9. YOUR SPIRITUAL ENERGY AND INNER FULFILMENT

10. WHAT YOU MOST NEED TO FOCUS ON IN THE YEAR AHEAD

11. YOUR MOST IMPORTANT LESSON FOR THE COMING YEAR

12. OVERALL, WHERE ARE YOU HEADED IN THE NEXT 12 MONTHS

JANUARY

WHEEL OF FORTUNE

As the new year begins, good fortune and luck are on your side. Everything is coming into alignment and you are riding the wave of success. Keep your mind open to all kinds of synchronicities and signs from the Universe. The magic of fate and destiny is behind you, and miracles are happening this month. However, be aware that change is inevitable and while you are experiencing success right now, it may not always be the way. This cycle shows why it is important to cherish the blissful moments in your life and make the most of them while they are within reach — because in a flash they could be gone.

 ### RITUAL: GRATITUDE FOR GOOD FORTUNE

Find the Wheel of Fortune card from your favorite deck and place it in front of you. Take a moment to look at the image and draw in the energy of this card. Then, in your journal, note down all the areas in your life where you are experiencing good fortune and luck right now. As you do this, feel every cell within your body fill with the golden light of success and abundance. Read through your list and as you do, give thanks to the Universe for supporting your success.

 ### CRYSTAL: GREEN AVENTURINE

To support the ritual, include a piece of Green Aventurine. It carries a deep connection to the Earth and helps to provide a vibration of soothing appreciation for all of life's blessings. Additionally, Green Aventurine is known as the "Stone of Opportunity" and is also one of the luckiest stones, which makes it a must-have for continuing your good fortunes.

 ### ASTROLOGICAL INFLUENCES

January 12: Saturn and Pluto conjunct in Capricorn. A Tower moment for structures that are no longer serving you. Create empowering routines with discipline.

January 20: Aquarius season begins. How will you take the disciplines and structures you've created and use them to create a sense of personal freedom? Meditate on the energies of The Star Tarot card.

INSIGHTS

JANUARY 10
FULL MOON IN CANCER

The full moon lunar eclipse in Cancer brings to fruition all that you've been working on in your emotional world. This is a potent time for nurturing and healing.

1. How have I nurtured my emotional self in the last 6 months?

2. Where in my life am I ready to heal?

3. How can I open my heart whilst maintaining healthy boundaries?

4. Which of my emotions are no longer serving my highest good?

5. What aspects of my Self need mothering now?

6. What do I need to release in order to trust life?

INSIGHTS

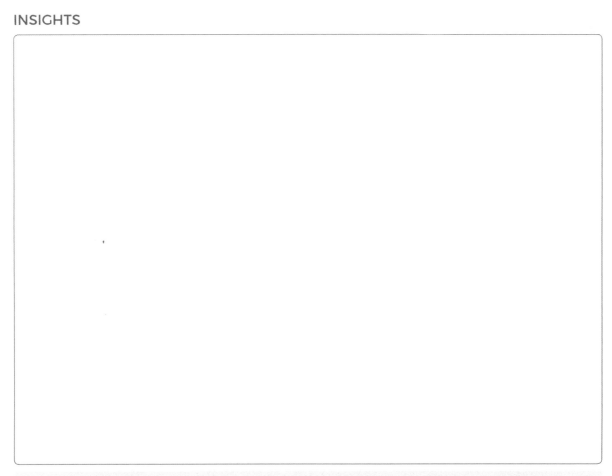

We love seeing you use your Biddy Tarot Planner! Completed this spread? Make sure you post a pic on Instagram and be sure to use the hashtag **#biddytarotplanner** so we can celebrate with you!

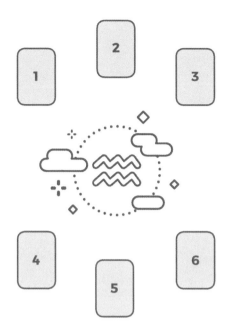

JANUARY 24

NEW MOON IN AQUARIUS

An Aquarius new moon is an opportunity to set out-of-the-box intentions — make your plans according to what you really want, not what other people think or expect.

1. What is my unique contribution in this world?

2. Where am I being called to speak my truth?

3. How can I break away from disempowering patterns of behavior?

4. How can I access my genius and think outside the box?

5. How can I connect meaningfully with my community?

6. What is my highest intention for my personal freedom?

INSIGHTS

JAN 01 WEDNESDAY   CARD OF THE DAY:

▷ INTENTION   ▷ REFLECTION

JAN 02 THURSDAY   CARD OF THE DAY:

▷ INTENTION   ▷ REFLECTION

JAN 03 FRIDAY   CARD OF THE DAY:

▷ INTENTION   ▷ REFLECTION

JAN 04 SATURDAY   CARD OF THE DAY:

▷ INTENTION   ▷ REFLECTION

JAN 05 SUNDAY   CARD OF THE DAY:

▷ INTENTION   ▷ REFLECTION

JAN 06 MONDAY   CARD OF THE DAY:

▷ INTENTION   ▷ REFLECTION

JAN 07 TUESDAY   CARD OF THE DAY:

▷ INTENTION   ▷ REFLECTION

JAN 08 WEDNESDAY   CARD OF THE DAY:

▷ INTENTION   ▷ REFLECTION

JAN 09 THURSDAY   CARD OF THE DAY:

▷ INTENTION   ▷ REFLECTION

JAN 10 FRIDAY   CARD OF THE DAY:

▷ INTENTION   ▷ REFLECTION

JAN 11 SATURDAY   CARD OF THE DAY:

▷ INTENTION   ▷ REFLECTION

JAN 12 SUNDAY   CARD OF THE DAY:

▷ INTENTION   ▷ REFLECTION

JAN 13 MONDAY   CARD OF THE DAY:

▷ INTENTION   ▷ REFLECTION

JAN 14 TUESDAY   CARD OF THE DAY:

▷ INTENTION   ▷ REFLECTION

JAN 15 WEDNESDAY   CARD OF THE DAY:

▷ INTENTION   ▷ REFLECTION

JAN 16 THURSDAY   CARD OF THE DAY:

▷ INTENTION   ▷ REFLECTION

JAN 17 FRIDAY   CARD OF THE DAY:

▷ INTENTION   ▷ REFLECTION

JAN 18 SATURDAY   CARD OF THE DAY:

▷ INTENTION   ▷ REFLECTION

JAN 19 SUNDAY   CARD OF THE DAY:

▷ INTENTION   ▷ REFLECTION

JAN 20 MONDAY   CARD OF THE DAY:

▷ INTENTION   ▷ REFLECTION

JAN 21 TUESDAY   CARD OF THE DAY:

▷ INTENTION   ▷ REFLECTION

JAN 22 WEDNESDAY CARD OF THE DAY:

▷ INTENTION   ▷ REFLECTION

JAN 23 THURSDAY CARD OF THE DAY:

▷ INTENTION   ▷ REFLECTION

JAN 24 FRIDAY CARD OF THE DAY:

▷ INTENTION   ▷ REFLECTION

JAN 25 SATURDAY CARD OF THE DAY:

▷ INTENTION   ▷ REFLECTION

JAN 26 SUNDAY CARD OF THE DAY:

▷ INTENTION   ▷ REFLECTION

JAN 27 MONDAY CARD OF THE DAY:

▷ INTENTION   ▷ REFLECTION

JAN 28 TUESDAY CARD OF THE DAY:

▷ INTENTION   ▷ REFLECTION

JAN 29 WEDNESDAY   CARD OF THE DAY:

▷ INTENTION   ▷ REFLECTION

JAN 30 THURSDAY   CARD OF THE DAY:

▷ INTENTION   ▷ REFLECTION

JAN 31 FRIDAY   CARD OF THE DAY:

▷ INTENTION   ▷ REFLECTION

INSIGHTS

FEBRUARY

THE CHARIOT

While the Wheel of Fortune in January was a sign of good luck and good fortune, the Chariot is a sign of creating your own good luck and fortune. You are channeling your inner power and fierce determination to bring your goals and dreams into fruition. You know that when you apply discipline, commitment and willpower to achieve your goals, you will succeed and there is no stopping you. Others may try to block you, distract you, or challenge you in the pursuit of your goal, but the Chariot is an invitation to draw upon your willpower and home in on what's essential to you, so you can push past the obstacles in your way to your ultimate success.

 ### RITUAL: DAILY INTENTIONS

Start your day with this Chariot-inspired morning ritual. Place the Chariot card in front of you and draw in its energy of pure focus and determination. Then contemplate your day. What 3 things do you want to accomplish today that will get you closer to your goals? Write these down in your journal. Next, consider what might stand in the way of you being able to complete these 3 things. How might you overcome these potential challenges? Write them down. To close the ritual, remind yourself of your 3 actions for today, knowing that you have what you need to overcome any challenges, and then start taking action, fueled by the strength of your commitment and dedication to do what it takes to achieve your goals.

 ### CRYSTAL: CHALCEDONY

Chalcedony helps to maintain balance and harmony in your life, while getting rid of any fears and anxieties. It clears the way for you to manifest your goals and bring your ideas to action. It is a grounding stone that protects you from negative influences and inspires optimism for the future.

 ### ASTROLOGICAL INFLUENCES

February 16: Mercury goes retrograde in Pisces. Re-evaluate your dreams, review your spiritual practices and renew your creativity.

February 18: Pisces season begins. Dream big and tune even more deeply into your intuition. Meditate on the energies of The Moon Tarot card.

INSIGHTS

FEBRUARY 9

FULL MOON IN LEO

Feel into the fullness of creativity and play and get ready to shine with the Leo full moon. Celebrate your warmth and your brilliance with this wonderful energy.

1. What have I created in the last 6 months?

2. How can I find joy in the present moment?

3. How am I shining my light in the world?

4. What creative pursuits will help center me?

5. Where can I be more spontaneous in my life?

6. What do I need to release in order to step into my power as a leader?

INSIGHTS

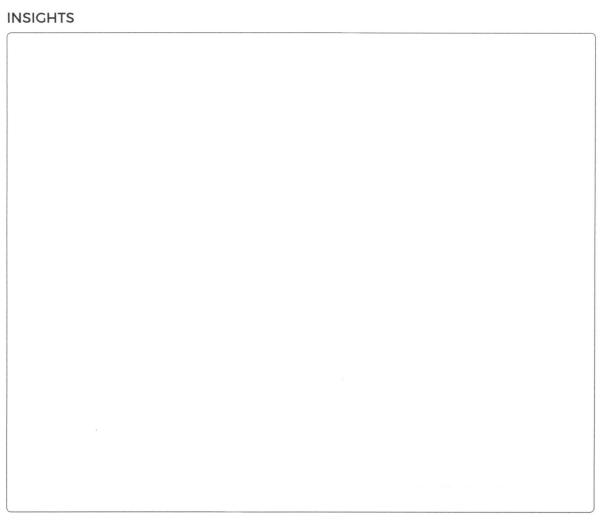

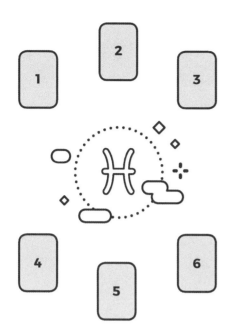

FEBRUARY 23

NEW MOON IN PISCES

Now is the time to let your imagination run wild and dream big. Tap into your intuition and set intentions to bring your visions to life.

1. What big dream do I want to bring to life?

2. How can I nurture my imagination each day?

3. How can I connect more deeply with my intuition?

4. What activities will bring me into a flow state?

5. What new creative projects am I called to begin now?

6. What is my highest intention for my spirituality?

INSIGHTS

On Instagram? Post a photo of your spread and your Tarot Planner with the hashtag **#biddytarotplanner** and we'll share with the Biddy Tarot community!

FEBRUARY | 35

FEB 01 SATURDAY

CARD OF THE DAY:

▷ INTENTION

▷ REFLECTION

FEB 02 SUNDAY

CARD OF THE DAY:

▷ INTENTION

▷ REFLECTION

FEB 03 MONDAY

CARD OF THE DAY:

▷ INTENTION

▷ REFLECTION

FEB 04 TUESDAY

CARD OF THE DAY:

▷ INTENTION

▷ REFLECTION

FEB 05 WEDNESDAY

CARD OF THE DAY:

▷ INTENTION

▷ REFLECTION

FEB 06 THURSDAY

CARD OF THE DAY:

▷ INTENTION

▷ REFLECTION

FEB 07 FRIDAY

CARD OF THE DAY:

▷ INTENTION

▷ REFLECTION

FEB 08 SATURDAY

CARD OF THE DAY:

▷ INTENTION

▷ REFLECTION

FEB 09 SUNDAY

CARD OF THE DAY:

▷ INTENTION

▷ REFLECTION

FEB 10 MONDAY

CARD OF THE DAY:

▷ INTENTION

▷ REFLECTION

FEB 11 TUESDAY

CARD OF THE DAY:

▷ INTENTION

▷ REFLECTION

FEB 12 WEDNESDAY

CARD OF THE DAY:

▷ INTENTION

▷ REFLECTION

FEB 13 THURSDAY

CARD OF THE DAY:

▷ INTENTION

▷ REFLECTION

FEB 14 FRIDAY

CARD OF THE DAY:

▷ INTENTION

▷ REFLECTION

FEB 15 SATURDAY

CARD OF THE DAY:

▷ INTENTION

▷ REFLECTION

FEB 16 SUNDAY

CARD OF THE DAY:

▷ INTENTION

▷ REFLECTION

FEB 17 MONDAY

CARD OF THE DAY:

▷ INTENTION

▷ REFLECTION

FEB 18 TUESDAY

CARD OF THE DAY:

▷ INTENTION

▷ REFLECTION

FEB 19 WEDNESDAY

CARD OF THE DAY:

▷ INTENTION

▷ REFLECTION

FEB 20 THURSDAY

CARD OF THE DAY:

▷ INTENTION

▷ REFLECTION

FEB 21 FRIDAY

CARD OF THE DAY:

▷ INTENTION

▷ REFLECTION

FEB 22   SATURDAY

CARD OF THE DAY:

▷ INTENTION

▷ REFLECTION

FEB 23   SUNDAY

CARD OF THE DAY:

▷ INTENTION

▷ REFLECTION

FEB 24   MONDAY

CARD OF THE DAY:

▷ INTENTION

▷ REFLECTION

FEB 25   TUESDAY

CARD OF THE DAY:

▷ INTENTION

▷ REFLECTION

FEB 26   WEDNESDAY

CARD OF THE DAY:

▷ INTENTION

▷ REFLECTION

FEB 27   THURSDAY

CARD OF THE DAY:

▷ INTENTION

▷ REFLECTION

FEB 28   FRIDAY

CARD OF THE DAY:

▷ INTENTION

▷ REFLECTION

FEB 29 SATURDAY

CARD OF THE DAY:

▷ INTENTION

▷ REFLECTION

INSIGHTS

MARCH

THE HANGED MAN

While the Chariot in February inspired focused action, the Hanged Man is now calling on you to slow down, surrender and hit 'pause' on your regular routine in March. This is your invitation to see the world from a different perspective and embrace new opportunities that will only become apparent once you slow down enough to see them. You may also be inspired (or forced) to put important projects on hold, even if it is completely inconvenient to do so. Don't keep pushing forward, hoping that more action will drive you to where you want to go. Instead, surrender to the opportunity to pause and view it as your chance to reassess and re-evaluate where you are on your path.

 ### RITUAL: RELEASE AND LET GO

Find a place outside where you can lay on the ground and not be disturbed. Before you lay down, find the Hanged Man in your favorite deck and draw in the energy of this powerful card. Then, lay yourself down comfortably on the ground. Feel yourself relax into the ground, and as you slowly let go and surrender, feel the ground supporting you and holding you. Then, look up into the sky and notice how different it looks from this perspective. Notice the clouds passing by in different shapes, and the gradients of color in the sky. Release anything that no longer serves you into the vastness that is the sky above you. When ready, slowly rise and write your insights into your journal.

 ### CRYSTAL: AMAZONITE

The soothing green color of Amazonite has a grounding effect on your soul and spirit that will aide in quieting your mind and allow new perspectives to come through.

 ### ASTROLOGICAL INFLUENCES

March 4: Mercury retrograde moves into Aquarius. Re-evaluate your perspective on the world. Mercury retrograde ends March 9.

March 20: Aries season and the astrological new year begin. Explore how you can take bold action to bring your desires to life. Meditate on the energies of The Emperor Tarot card.

March 21: Saturn in Aquarius. Feelings of restriction and potential conflict between freedom and discipline. How can you use discipline to create ultimate freedom?

INSIGHTS

FULL MOON IN VIRGO

Honor the ways you are serving the world and the places you are creating order from chaos at this Virgo full moon.

1. What have I mastered in the last 6 months?

2. What gift do I offer the world through service?

3. How am I growing into my potential?

4. How can I create a sense of order in my environment?

5. What practical matters can I focus on for my emotional fulfillment?

6. What do I need to release in order to love myself unconditionally?

INSIGHTS

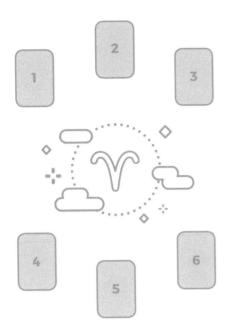

MARCH 24
NEW MOON IN ARIES

Use the extra dose of Aries courage to set bold intentions at this new moon. What would you do if you knew you would succeed?

1. How can I shape my life to align with my true desires?

2. Where do I need to assert myself to feel emotionally secure?

3. What new experiences will heighten my self-confidence?

4. What courageous action do I need to take to achieve my goals?

5. How can I handle conflict effectively?

6. What is my highest intention for my personal power?

INSIGHTS

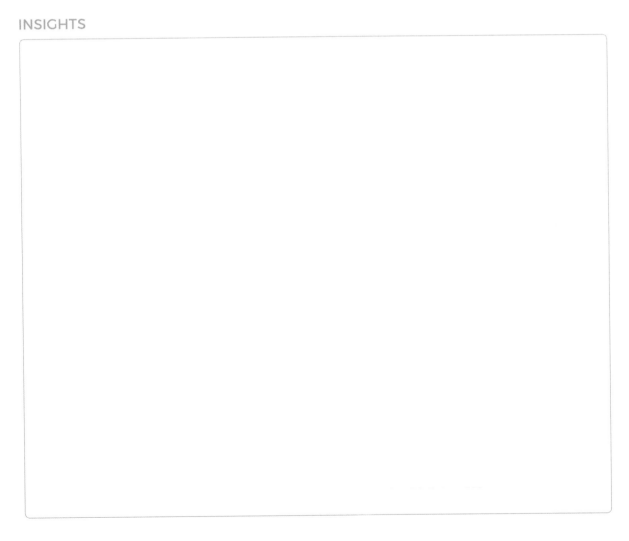

MAR 01 SUNDAY

CARD OF THE DAY:

▷ INTENTION

▷ REFLECTION

MAR 02 MONDAY

CARD OF THE DAY:

▷ INTENTION

▷ REFLECTION

MAR 03 TUESDAY

CARD OF THE DAY:

▷ INTENTION

▷ REFLECTION

MAR 04 WEDNESDAY

CARD OF THE DAY:

▷ INTENTION

▷ REFLECTION

MAR 05 THURSDAY

CARD OF THE DAY:

▷ INTENTION

▷ REFLECTION

MAR 06 FRIDAY

CARD OF THE DAY:

▷ INTENTION

▷ REFLECTION

MAR 07 SATURDAY

CARD OF THE DAY:

▷ INTENTION

▷ REFLECTION

MAR 08 SUNDAY
CARD OF THE DAY:

▷ INTENTION

▷ REFLECTION

MAR 09 MONDAY
CARD OF THE DAY:

▷ INTENTION

▷ REFLECTION

MAR 10 TUESDAY
CARD OF THE DAY:

▷ INTENTION

▷ REFLECTION

MAR 11 WEDNESDAY
CARD OF THE DAY:

▷ INTENTION

▷ REFLECTION

MAR 12 THURSDAY
CARD OF THE DAY:

▷ INTENTION

▷ REFLECTION

MAR 13 FRIDAY
CARD OF THE DAY:

▷ INTENTION

▷ REFLECTION

MAR 14 SATURDAY
CARD OF THE DAY:

▷ INTENTION

▷ REFLECTION

MAR 15 SUNDAY   CARD OF THE DAY:

▷ INTENTION   ▷ REFLECTION

MAR 16 MONDAY   CARD OF THE DAY:

▷ INTENTION   ▷ REFLECTION

MAR 17 TUESDAY   CARD OF THE DAY:

▷ INTENTION   ▷ REFLECTION

MAR 18 WEDNESDAY   CARD OF THE DAY:

▷ INTENTION   ▷ REFLECTION

MAR 19 THURSDAY   CARD OF THE DAY:

▷ INTENTION   ▷ REFLECTION

MAR 20 FRIDAY   CARD OF THE DAY:

▷ INTENTION   ▷ REFLECTION

MAR 21 SATURDAY   CARD OF THE DAY:

▷ INTENTION   ▷ REFLECTION

MAR 22 SUNDAY

CARD OF THE DAY:

▷ INTENTION

▷ REFLECTION

MAR 23 MONDAY

CARD OF THE DAY:

▷ INTENTION

▷ REFLECTION

MAR 24 TUESDAY

CARD OF THE DAY:

▷ INTENTION

▷ REFLECTION

MAR 25 WEDNESDAY

CARD OF THE DAY:

▷ INTENTION

▷ REFLECTION

MAR 26 THURSDAY

CARD OF THE DAY:

▷ INTENTION

▷ REFLECTION

MAR 27 FRIDAY

CARD OF THE DAY:

▷ INTENTION

▷ REFLECTION

MAR 28 SATURDAY

CARD OF THE DAY:

▷ INTENTION

▷ REFLECTION

MAR 29 SUNDAY
CARD OF THE DAY:

▷ INTENTION

▷ REFLECTION

MAR 30 MONDAY
CARD OF THE DAY:

▷ INTENTION

▷ REFLECTION

MAR 31 TUESDAY
CARD OF THE DAY:

▷ INTENTION

▷ REFLECTION

INSIGHTS

SPRING EQUINOX SPREAD

Spring Equinox (March 20 in the Northern Hemisphere; September 23 in the Southern Hemisphere) honors new growth and opportunity. The seeds have been planted and, nurtured by the rain, they are now emerging from the earth into the brightness of the sunlight, blossoming into beautiful flowers, fruit and foliage. Spring time is filled with color, scents and a feeling of excitement and anticipation of what's to come.

This is the perfect time to explore new possibilities, start new projects, and truly blossom. Use the following Tarot spread around the time of the Spring Equinox to connect with this sacred energy.

1. What has emerged for me over the Winter period?

2. What lesson have I learned?

3. What new seeds are beginning to sprout?

4. How can I nurture these new opportunities?

5. How am I truly blossoming?

6. How can I best embrace the Spring energy?

INSIGHTS

INSIGHTS

SPRING EQUINOX INTENTIONS

Holding the energy and insight of your Spring Equinox Tarot Reading, set your intentions for the next three months:

APRIL

THE EMPRESS

The Empress invites you to connect with your Divine feminine energy. Prioritize pleasure and create full-sensory experiences through taste, touch, sound, smell and sight. Find beauty in all things and enjoy the abundance that life has to offer. April also brings a period of growth, in which all you have dreamed of is now coming to fruition. Take a moment to reflect on the bounty that surrounds you and offer gratitude for all you have created so you can continue to build on this energy and create even more abundance in your life.

 ### RITUAL: THE EMPRESS BATH

This month, prioritize pleasure with an Empress Bath. Draw a warm bath and as it fills, add two cups of Epsom Salt, a handful of fresh or dried flowers (e.g. rose petals or buds, lavender, or jasmine), and 10 drops of essential oils (e.g. ylang ylang, sandalwood, rose, or frankincense). Around your bath, place your favorite crystals and candles, and turn on some relaxing music. As you enter your Empress Bath, set an intention, blessing or prayer of self-love. Gently ease yourself into the warm water, and pour the water over your arms, chest, and head. Then relax and enjoy the beauty and pleasure of this sacred bath.

 ### CRYSTAL: MOONSTONE

Nurture yourself with the hopeful, soothing and inspirational energy of Moonstone. Unlock your inner goddess and allow the power of the Moonstone to support you. Just like the Moon, even if you can't see it – the energy of Moonstone is there, pulling on your inner tides and setting your own natural rhythms back in balance.

☿ ASTROLOGICAL INFLUENCES

April 4: Jupiter and Pluto conjunct in Capricorn. Get clear on what you truly want as this energy will give you the focus and drive to make it happen.

April 19: Taurus season begins. Focus on activities and spaces that bring you peace. Meditate on the energies of The Hierophant Tarot card.

April 25: Pluto retrograde. A chance to review your deepest desires and impulses, creating more alignment in your life.

INSIGHTS

APRIL 8
FULL MOON
IN LIBRA

The Libra full moon invites you to revel in beauty and release the things that negatively impact your sense of harmony and balance.

1. Where have I created harmony in my life in the last 6 months?

2. How can I create more balance in my relationships?

3. Where do I need to be more objective in my life?

4. How can I cooperate more graciously with others?

5. What beauty surrounds me now?

6. What do I need to release in order to feel balanced?

INSIGHTS

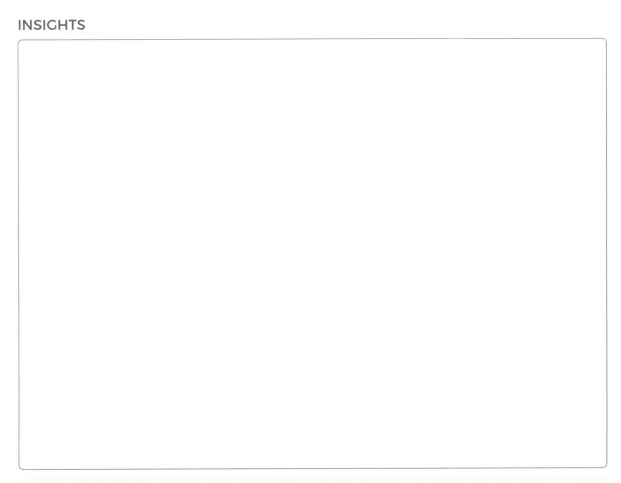

We love seeing you use your Biddy Tarot Planner! Completed this spread? Make sure you post a pic on Instagram and be sure to use the hashtag **#biddytarotplanner** so we can celebrate with you!

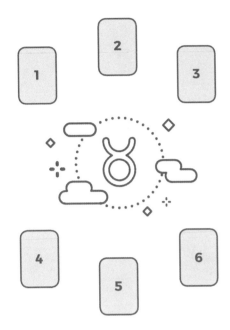

NEW MOON IN TAURUS

With the new moon in Taurus you have the chance to become conscious about creating peaceful and pleasurable experiences in your life. Use this energy to develop empowering new habits.

1. How can I embody peace and tranquility in my life?

2. What does nature have to teach me at this time?

3. How can I savor the simple pleasures in life?

4. What new, empowering habits can I introduce into my days?

5. What activities will help me become more grounded in my physical self?

6. What is my highest intention for my inner contentment?

INSIGHTS

APR 01 WEDNESDAY   CARD OF THE DAY:

▷ INTENTION   ▷ REFLECTION

APR 02 THURSDAY   CARD OF THE DAY:

▷ INTENTION   ▷ REFLECTION

APR 03 FRIDAY   CARD OF THE DAY:

▷ INTENTION   ▷ REFLECTION

APR 04 SATURDAY   CARD OF THE DAY:

▷ INTENTION   ▷ REFLECTION

APR 05 SUNDAY   CARD OF THE DAY:

▷ INTENTION   ▷ REFLECTION

APR 06 MONDAY   CARD OF THE DAY:

▷ INTENTION   ▷ REFLECTION

APR 07 TUESDAY   CARD OF THE DAY:

▷ INTENTION   ▷ REFLECTION

APR 08   WEDNESDAY   CARD OF THE DAY:

▷ INTENTION   ▷ REFLECTION

APR 09   THURSDAY   CARD OF THE DAY:

▷ INTENTION   ▷ REFLECTION

APR 10   FRIDAY   CARD OF THE DAY:

▷ INTENTION   ▷ REFLECTION

APR 11   SATURDAY   CARD OF THE DAY:

▷ INTENTION   ▷ REFLECTION

APR 12   SUNDAY   CARD OF THE DAY:

▷ INTENTION   ▷ REFLECTION

APR 13   MONDAY   CARD OF THE DAY:

▷ INTENTION   ▷ REFLECTION

APR 14   TUESDAY   CARD OF THE DAY:

▷ INTENTION   ▷ REFLECTION

APR 15   WEDNESDAY   CARD OF THE DAY:

▷ INTENTION

▷ REFLECTION

APR 16   THURSDAY   CARD OF THE DAY:

▷ INTENTION

▷ REFLECTION

APR 17   FRIDAY   CARD OF THE DAY:

▷ INTENTION

▷ REFLECTION

APR 18   SATURDAY   CARD OF THE DAY:

▷ INTENTION

▷ REFLECTION

APR 19   SUNDAY   CARD OF THE DAY:

▷ INTENTION

▷ REFLECTION

APR 20   MONDAY   CARD OF THE DAY:

▷ INTENTION

▷ REFLECTION

APR 21   TUESDAY   CARD OF THE DAY:

▷ INTENTION

▷ REFLECTION

APR 22 WEDNESDAY   CARD OF THE DAY:

▷ INTENTION   ▷ REFLECTION

APR 23 THURSDAY   CARD OF THE DAY:

▷ INTENTION   ▷ REFLECTION

APR 24 FRIDAY   CARD OF THE DAY:

▷ INTENTION   ▷ REFLECTION

APR 25 SATURDAY   CARD OF THE DAY:

▷ INTENTION   ▷ REFLECTION

APR 26 SUNDAY   CARD OF THE DAY:

▷ INTENTION   ▷ REFLECTION

APR 27 MONDAY   CARD OF THE DAY:

▷ INTENTION   ▷ REFLECTION

APR 28 TUESDAY   CARD OF THE DAY:

▷ INTENTION   ▷ REFLECTION

APR 29 WEDNESDAY

CARD OF THE DAY:

▷ INTENTION

▷ REFLECTION

APR 30 THURSDAY

CARD OF THE DAY:

▷ INTENTION

▷ REFLECTION

INSIGHTS

MAY

THE HIGH PRIESTESS

HIGH PRIESTESS

This month, you are invited to connect deeply with your intuition and your Higher Self. The veil between you and the underworld is very thin right now and you have the opportunity to access the knowledge that is deep within your soul. Access your inner wisdom and your divine feminine energy through meditation, visualization, shamanic journeying, and being part of a spiritual community. The answers you are seeking will come from within, from your deepest truth and 'knowing'. Allow the High Priestess to become your guide as you venture deep into your subconscious mind and access this inner wisdom.

RITUAL: INTUITIVE MEDITATION

Make a commitment this month to sit in meditation daily, even if it's just for 5 minutes. Before you begin your meditation, hold the High Priestess card in front of you, and say out loud, "I call upon the intuitive power and knowledge of the High Priestess and my Higher Self to guide me." Then, close your eyes and sit in silence for a period of time. Start by simply focusing on your breathing. Then, with a quiet, curious mind, be open to receive any new insights that begin to flow from your intuition, perhaps as images, words, thoughts, feelings, or a general 'knowing'. Don't force it – just allow it to flow. When you're ready, open your eyes and write down your insights.

CRYSTAL: LABRADORITE

Labradorite awakens you to your inner consciousness, taking you deep within to access your Higher Self, your inner being and your source of all wisdom. It is a powerful stone that aids in intuition, psychic abilities, clairvoyance and a deeper connection to one's true Self.

ASTROLOGICAL INFLUENCES

A powerful retrograde season begins with Saturn, Venus and Jupiter all turning retrograde within days of each other (**May 11**, **13** and **14** respectively). This is a time to review your values and assess the structures in your life. Are they serving your higher purpose?

May 20: Gemini season begins. Communication and social activity could be heightened, and the energy is ripe for learning something new. Meditate on the energies of The Lovers Tarot card.

INSIGHTS

MAY 7
FULL MOON IN SCORPIO

Intense energies surround the Scorpio full moon, creating an ideal time for shadow work and transformational activities. Use this energy to release anything that no longer resonates with your true self.

1. What have I discovered about who I am in the last 6 months?

2. How can I more fully live every moment?

3. Where do I need to be more present?

4. What intense emotions are coming up for me now?

5. How can I cultivate my passions?

6. What do I need to release in order to experience deep transformation?

INSIGHTS

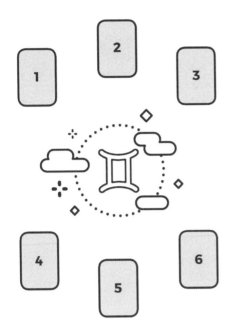

MAY 22
NEW MOON IN GEMINI

A fresh new moon in Gemini brings a sense of lightness after the last full moon. Set intentions around what you want to learn and teach, and how you can communicate for maximum effect.

1. How can I enhance my perceptions of the world around me?

2. What new areas am I curious about now?

3. What am I committed to learning in the next 6 months?

4. Where do I need to verbalize my emotions?

5. How can I further open my mind at this time?

6. What is my highest intention for my communications?

INSIGHTS

MAY 01 FRIDAY   CARD OF THE DAY:

▷ INTENTION   ▷ REFLECTION

MAY 02 SATURDAY   CARD OF THE DAY:

▷ INTENTION   ▷ REFLECTION

MAY 03 SUNDAY   CARD OF THE DAY:

▷ INTENTION   ▷ REFLECTION

MAY 04 MONDAY   CARD OF THE DAY:

▷ INTENTION   ▷ REFLECTION

MAY 05 TUESDAY   CARD OF THE DAY:

▷ INTENTION   ▷ REFLECTION

MAY 06 WEDNESDAY   CARD OF THE DAY:

▷ INTENTION   ▷ REFLECTION

MAY 07 THURSDAY   CARD OF THE DAY:

▷ INTENTION   ▷ REFLECTION

MAY 08 FRIDAY

CARD OF THE DAY:

▷ INTENTION

▷ REFLECTION

MAY 09 SATURDAY

CARD OF THE DAY:

▷ INTENTION

▷ REFLECTION

MAY 10 SUNDAY

CARD OF THE DAY:

▷ INTENTION

▷ REFLECTION

MAY 11 MONDAY

CARD OF THE DAY:

▷ INTENTION

▷ REFLECTION

MAY 12 TUESDAY

CARD OF THE DAY:

▷ INTENTION

▷ REFLECTION

MAY 13 WEDNESDAY

CARD OF THE DAY:

▷ INTENTION

▷ REFLECTION

MAY 14 THURSDAY

CARD OF THE DAY:

▷ INTENTION

▷ REFLECTION

MAY 15 FRIDAY

CARD OF THE DAY:

▷ INTENTION

▷ REFLECTION

MAY 16 SATURDAY

CARD OF THE DAY:

▷ INTENTION

▷ REFLECTION

MAY 17 SUNDAY

CARD OF THE DAY:

▷ INTENTION

▷ REFLECTION

MAY 18 MONDAY

CARD OF THE DAY:

▷ INTENTION

▷ REFLECTION

MAY 19 TUESDAY

CARD OF THE DAY:

▷ INTENTION

▷ REFLECTION

MAY 20 WEDNESDAY

CARD OF THE DAY:

▷ INTENTION

▷ REFLECTION

MAY 21 THURSDAY

CARD OF THE DAY:

▷ INTENTION

▷ REFLECTION

MAY 22 FRIDAY

CARD OF THE DAY:

▷ INTENTION

▷ REFLECTION

MAY 23 SATURDAY

CARD OF THE DAY:

▷ INTENTION

▷ REFLECTION

MAY 24 SUNDAY

CARD OF THE DAY:

▷ INTENTION

▷ REFLECTION

MAY 25 MONDAY

CARD OF THE DAY:

▷ INTENTION

▷ REFLECTION

MAY 26 TUESDAY

CARD OF THE DAY:

▷ INTENTION

▷ REFLECTION

MAY 27 WEDNESDAY

CARD OF THE DAY:

▷ INTENTION

▷ REFLECTION

MAY 28 THURSDAY

CARD OF THE DAY:

▷ INTENTION

▷ REFLECTION

MAY 29 FRIDAY

CARD OF THE DAY:

▷ INTENTION

▷ REFLECTION

MAY 30 SATURDAY

CARD OF THE DAY:

▷ INTENTION

▷ REFLECTION

MAY 31 SUNDAY

CARD OF THE DAY:

▷ INTENTION

▷ REFLECTION

INSIGHTS

JUNE

THE STAR

This month holds beauty, promise and inspiration for you. Right now, anything is possible, and the magic is flowing around you. Your heart is filled with renewed hope and your soul is being uplifted to the highest of highs as you realize that your dreams really can come true. Allow yourself to dream, to aspire, to elevate in any way possible so that you can truly reach the stars. They are right here waiting for you. You may also want to find or rediscover a sense of meaning, inspiration, or purpose in your life. You are making some significant changes in your life in June, transforming yourself from the old you to the new you and, in doing so, you are choosing the highest version of yourself.

RITUAL: WISH UPON A STAR

In this month's ritual, you are invited to 'wish upon a star'. On the next starry night, take out the Star card from your favorite Tarot deck and connect with its energy. Then, go outside and look up into the stars and the Universe above. Feel your heart and your mind expand into this infinite potential. Then, make a wish. Wish something that is so big, so dreamy, and so 'out there'. Hold your wish's energy in your heart, then hand it over to the Universe. The Universe has your back!

CRYSTAL: CLEAR QUARTZ

Clear Quartz is the perfect stone to support you in gaining the clarity that you need to go within and focus on exactly what you want to wish for. If you can find a quartz that has a rainbow inclusion, it will inspire you to realize what it is you need in order to be the best possible version of yourself.

ASTROLOGICAL INFLUENCES

June 18: Mercury Retrograde in Cancer. Review your emotional world and the ways you nurture yourself and others.

June 20: Cancer season begins. Meditate on the energies of The Chariot Tarot card.

June 23: Neptune retrograde. Turn inwards and re-evaluate your spiritual path and life vision.

June 25: Venus turns direct. Issues on love and money may become clearer now.

INSIGHTS

JUNE 5

FULL MOON IN SAGITTARIUS

Ideals and visions are heightened with this full moon lunar eclipse in Sagittarius. Tap into this expansive energy and release anything that is keeping you small.

1. How has my awareness expanded in the last 6 months?

2. How am I progressing towards my goals?

3. Which beliefs and ideals am I passionate about now?

4. Where can I be more open and truthful in my life?

5. What is my guiding vision for the future?

6. What do I need to release in order to feel free?

INSIGHTS

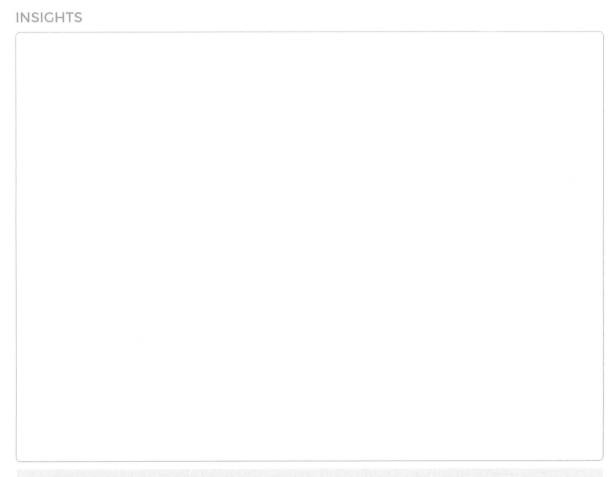

Don't forget to snap a pic of your reading and share on IG using the hashtag **#biddytarotplanner**. We love seeing you using your Biddy Tarot Planner in action and can't wait to celebrate with you!

68 | 2020 BIDDY TAROT PLANNER

JUNE 21

NEW MOON IN CANCER

The moon obscures the sun in the new moon solar eclipse in Cancer, calling into question the ways in which your emotions may be blocking you from shining your light. How can you integrate your private self with your public self?

1. What new emotions are emerging for me?

2. Where do I feel most vulnerable in my life right now?

3. How can I create more emotional safety in my relationships?

4. How can I nurture and care for myself?

5. How can I create a sacred space in my home?

6. What is my highest intention for my emotional wellbeing?

INSIGHTS

JUN 01 MONDAY   CARD OF THE DAY:

▷ INTENTION

▷ REFLECTION

JUN 02 TUESDAY   CARD OF THE DAY:

▷ INTENTION

▷ REFLECTION

JUN 03 WEDNESDAY   CARD OF THE DAY:

▷ INTENTION

▷ REFLECTION

JUN 04 THURSDAY   CARD OF THE DAY:

▷ INTENTION

▷ REFLECTION

JUN 05 FRIDAY   CARD OF THE DAY:

▷ INTENTION

▷ REFLECTION

JUN 06 SATURDAY   CARD OF THE DAY:

▷ INTENTION

▷ REFLECTION

JUN 07 SUNDAY   CARD OF THE DAY:

▷ INTENTION

▷ REFLECTION

JUN 08 MONDAY

CARD OF THE DAY:

▷ INTENTION

▷ REFLECTION

JUN 09 TUESDAY

CARD OF THE DAY:

▷ INTENTION

▷ REFLECTION

JUN 10 WEDNESDAY

CARD OF THE DAY:

▷ INTENTION

▷ REFLECTION

JUN 11 THURSDAY

CARD OF THE DAY:

▷ INTENTION

▷ REFLECTION

JUN 12 FRIDAY

CARD OF THE DAY:

▷ INTENTION

▷ REFLECTION

JUN 13 SATURDAY

CARD OF THE DAY:

▷ INTENTION

▷ REFLECTION

JUN 14 SUNDAY

CARD OF THE DAY:

▷ INTENTION

▷ REFLECTION

JUN 15   MONDAY   CARD OF THE DAY:

▷ INTENTION   ▷ REFLECTION

JUN 16   TUESDAY   CARD OF THE DAY:

▷ INTENTION   ▷ REFLECTION

JUN 17   WEDNESDAY   CARD OF THE DAY:

▷ INTENTION   ▷ REFLECTION

JUN 18   THURSDAY   CARD OF THE DAY:

▷ INTENTION   ▷ REFLECTION

JUN 19   FRIDAY   CARD OF THE DAY:

▷ INTENTION   ▷ REFLECTION

JUN 20   SATURDAY   CARD OF THE DAY:

▷ INTENTION   ▷ REFLECTION

JUN 21   SUNDAY   CARD OF THE DAY:

▷ INTENTION   ▷ REFLECTION

JUN 22 MONDAY   CARD OF THE DAY:

▷ INTENTION   ▷ REFLECTION

JUN 23 TUESDAY   CARD OF THE DAY:

▷ INTENTION   ▷ REFLECTION

JUN 24 WEDNESDAY   CARD OF THE DAY:

▷ INTENTION   ▷ REFLECTION

JUN 25 THURSDAY   CARD OF THE DAY:

▷ INTENTION   ▷ REFLECTION

JUN 26 FRIDAY   CARD OF THE DAY:

▷ INTENTION   ▷ REFLECTION

JUN 27 SATURDAY   CARD OF THE DAY:

▷ INTENTION   ▷ REFLECTION

JUN 28 SUNDAY   CARD OF THE DAY:

▷ INTENTION   ▷ REFLECTION

JUN 29 MONDAY   CARD OF THE DAY:

▷ INTENTION   ▷ REFLECTION

JUN 30 TUESDAY   CARD OF THE DAY:

▷ INTENTION   ▷ REFLECTION

INSIGHTS

SUMMER SOLSTICE SPREAD

Summer Solstice (June 20 in the Northern Hemisphere; December 21 in the Southern Hemisphere) is the time to shine and be seen. Be ready to step into the spotlight and express your true self to the world. Bask in the sunrays and allow yourself to be filled with light as you feel a sense of accomplishment and fulfilment.

Watch as your projects come into full effect and you are energized to take action on the new opportunities that arose during the Spring time. Use the following Tarot spread around the time of the Summer Solstice to connect with this sacred energy.

1. What new opportunities have emerged over the Spring?

2. How can I bring my current projects to fruition?

3. What is expanding in my life right now?

4. What blessings am I receiving?

5. What truly fulfils me?

6. How can I shine my light in the world?

INSIGHTS

INSIGHTS

SUMMER SOLSTICE INTENTIONS

Holding the energy and insight of your Summer Solstice Tarot Reading, set your intentions for the next three months:

JULY

THE HIEROPHANT

This month, you have the opportunity to learn from a wise teacher who nurtures your spiritual awareness and helps you access the Divine by understanding its traditions and core principles. This teacher may appear as a coach, mentor, guru, author, spiritual leader, friend or partner. Be open to receive their 'tried and tested' advice about what does and doesn't work, and tap into their core beliefs, mindset and philosophies, as these will guide you along your personal path. You may find yourself not only in the student role, but also the teacher, sharing your own wisdoms with others and being a beacon of light and inspiration.

 ### RITUAL: HONORING YOUR TEACHERS

First, connect with the energy of the Hierophant Tarot card, feeling into the wise advice this teacher has to share with you. Then, write down the names of all the people who have supported you in your spiritual awareness and growth. What lessons have they taught you? What sage advice did they share? How have they contributed to your spiritual development? When your list is complete, reflect on each person, feeling their energy within your heart, and give thanks for the lessons they have taught you. You may even feel compelled to write a letter of gratitude to those who have inspired you the most.

 ### CRYSTAL: CELESTITE

Celestite is the "Teacher of the New Age" and is the perfect stone to support you along your path of spiritual awareness. A high-vibrational stone, Celestite will activate the Third Eye Chakra, allowing you to access your guides and all the knowledge they have to share with you.

⊘ ASTROLOGICAL INFLUENCES

July 12: Mercury retrograde ends.

July 22: Leo season begins. Time to shine! Use the fiery Leo energy to create a life and image you love. Meditate on The Strength Tarot card.

INSIGHTS

JULY 5
FULL MOON IN CAPRICORN

The full moon lunar eclipse in Capricorn is a powerful time to reflect on your achievements. Where have you stood in integrity and built something you're proud of?

1. What have I achieved in the last 6 months?

2. What am I yet to achieve?

3. What does 'full expansion' look like for me?

4. What foundations do I need to establish to support my success?

5. What is a non-negotiable for me right now?

6. What do I need to release in order to feel successful?

INSIGHTS

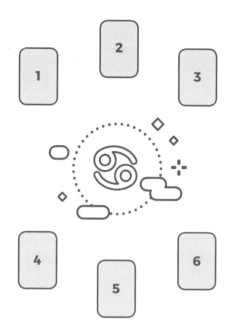

JULY 20

NEW MOON IN CANCER

If there were ever a time to make conscious choices about how you feel day to day, the new moon in Cancer would be that time. Dive into your emotional world and set empowering intentions around how you want to feel.

1. What new emotions are emerging for me?

2. Where do I feel most vulnerable in my life right now?

3. How can I create more emotional safety in my relationships?

4. How can I nurture and care for myself?

5. How can I create a sacred space in my home?

6. What is my highest intention for my emotional wellbeing?

INSIGHTS

On Instagram? Post a photo of your spread and your Tarot Planner with the hashtag **#biddytarotplanner** and we'll share with the Biddy Tarot community!

JUL 01 WEDNESDAY   CARD OF THE DAY:

▷ INTENTION   ▷ REFLECTION

JUL 02 THURSDAY   CARD OF THE DAY:

▷ INTENTION   ▷ REFLECTION

JUL 03 FRIDAY   CARD OF THE DAY:

▷ INTENTION   ▷ REFLECTION

JUL 04 SATURDAY   CARD OF THE DAY:

▷ INTENTION   ▷ REFLECTION

JUL 05 SUNDAY   CARD OF THE DAY:

▷ INTENTION   ▷ REFLECTION

JUL 06 MONDAY   CARD OF THE DAY:

▷ INTENTION   ▷ REFLECTION

JUL 07 TUESDAY   CARD OF THE DAY:

▷ INTENTION   ▷ REFLECTION

JUL 08   WEDNESDAY

CARD OF THE DAY:

▷ INTENTION

▷ REFLECTION

JUL 09   THURSDAY

CARD OF THE DAY:

▷ INTENTION

▷ REFLECTION

JUL 10   FRIDAY

CARD OF THE DAY:

▷ INTENTION

▷ REFLECTION

JUL 11   SATURDAY

CARD OF THE DAY:

▷ INTENTION

▷ REFLECTION

JUL 12   SUNDAY

CARD OF THE DAY:

▷ INTENTION

▷ REFLECTION

JUL 13   MONDAY

CARD OF THE DAY:

▷ INTENTION

▷ REFLECTION

JUL 14   TUESDAY

CARD OF THE DAY:

▷ INTENTION

▷ REFLECTION

JUL 15   WEDNESDAY   CARD OF THE DAY:

▷ INTENTION   ▷ REFLECTION

JUL 16   THURSDAY   CARD OF THE DAY:

▷ INTENTION   ▷ REFLECTION

JUL 17   FRIDAY   CARD OF THE DAY:

▷ INTENTION   ▷ REFLECTION

JUL 18   SATURDAY   CARD OF THE DAY:

▷ INTENTION   ▷ REFLECTION

JUL 19   SUNDAY   CARD OF THE DAY:

▷ INTENTION   ▷ REFLECTION

JUL 20   MONDAY   CARD OF THE DAY:

▷ INTENTION   ▷ REFLECTION

JUL 21   TUESDAY   CARD OF THE DAY:

▷ INTENTION   ▷ REFLECTION

JUL 22   WEDNESDAY   CARD OF THE DAY:

▷ INTENTION   ▷ REFLECTION

JUL 23   THURSDAY   CARD OF THE DAY:

▷ INTENTION   ▷ REFLECTION

JUL 24   FRIDAY   CARD OF THE DAY:

▷ INTENTION   ▷ REFLECTION

JUL 25   SATURDAY   CARD OF THE DAY:

▷ INTENTION   ▷ REFLECTION

JUL 26   SUNDAY   CARD OF THE DAY:

▷ INTENTION   ▷ REFLECTION

JUL 27   MONDAY   CARD OF THE DAY:

▷ INTENTION   ▷ REFLECTION

JUL 28   TUESDAY   CARD OF THE DAY:

▷ INTENTION   ▷ REFLECTION

JUL 29 WEDNESDAY   CARD OF THE DAY:

▷ INTENTION   ▷ REFLECTION

JUL 30 THURSDAY   CARD OF THE DAY:

▷ INTENTION   ▷ REFLECTION

JUL 31 FRIDAY   CARD OF THE DAY:

▷ INTENTION   ▷ REFLECTION

INSIGHTS

AUGUST

THE HERMIT

This month, you are invited to retreat from everyday life and embark on a spiritual journey to bring deep awareness to your life path. Draw your energy and attention inward and find the answers you seek, deep within your soul. You will come to realize that your most profound sense of truth and knowledge is within you, and not in the distractions of the outside world. August is the perfect time to go on a weekend retreat or sacred pilgrimage, anything in which you can contemplate your motivations, personal values and principles, and get closer to your authentic self. You may also be at a pivotal point in your life and considering a new direction, using meditation, contemplation, and self-examination to re-evaluate your personal goals and change your overall course.

RITUAL: SPIRITUAL RETREAT

Choose a day (or weekend, week, or even month) where you can retreat from your everyday life and experience a period of solitude and reflection. You may go on a hike, travel to a remote location or book an AirBnB – somewhere you won't be disturbed and where you can have an extended period on your own. Take along your journal, Tarot and oracle cards, and spend the day simply reflecting on your life and what you have learned along the way. Honor the stillness from within and reconnect with your inner guiding light to show you the way forward.

CRYSTAL: LAPIS LAZULI

Known as the "Stone of Truth", Lapis Lazuli will aid you in discovering your own personal truths. Enhancing inner-wisdom and good judgement that will be helpful as you get closer to your authentic self and break down the barriers that are holding you back.

ASTROLOGICAL INFLUENCES

August 15: Uranus retrograde in Taurus. The next 5 months are a good time to reassess your ideas of your own worth and truly understand your unique value.

August 22: Virgo season begins. This is a great time to establish empowering routines and focus on mastering a skill. Meditate on The Hermit Tarot card.

INSIGHTS

AUGUST 3

FULL MOON IN AQUARIUS

The full moon in Aquarius invites you to explore the culmination of your efforts in the areas of personal freedom, community and progress towards your heart-centered goals.

1. What unique contribution to the world have I made in the last 6 months?

2. How can I make a difference to my community?

3. How can I grow and expand my friendships?

4. How can I bring light to my truth?

5. What does true freedom look like for me?

6. What do I need to release to create more freedom in my life?

INSIGHTS

AUGUST 19

NEW MOON IN LEO

Your creations and passions are coming into focus with the new moon in Leo. A time for setting courageous intentions about how you want to show up in the world.

1. What does my heart want to create?

2. What new aspects of myself am I expressing?

3. How can I manifest my deepest desires?

4. How do I want to be seen?

5. How can I lead from the heart?

6. What is my highest intention for my creations?

INSIGHTS

On Instagram? Post a photo of your spread and your Tarot Planner with the hashtag **#biddytarotplanner** and we'll share with the Biddy Tarot community!

AUGUST | 87

AUG 01 SATURDAY
CARD OF THE DAY:

▷ INTENTION

▷ REFLECTION

AUG 02 SUNDAY
CARD OF THE DAY:

▷ INTENTION

▷ REFLECTION

AUG 03 MONDAY
CARD OF THE DAY:

▷ INTENTION

▷ REFLECTION

AUG 04 TUESDAY
CARD OF THE DAY:

▷ INTENTION

▷ REFLECTION

AUG 05 WEDNESDAY
CARD OF THE DAY:

▷ INTENTION

▷ REFLECTION

AUG 06 THURSDAY
CARD OF THE DAY:

▷ INTENTION

▷ REFLECTION

AUG 07 FRIDAY
CARD OF THE DAY:

▷ INTENTION

▷ REFLECTION

AUG 08 SATURDAY

CARD OF THE DAY:

▷ INTENTION

▷ REFLECTION

AUG 09 SUNDAY

CARD OF THE DAY:

▷ INTENTION

▷ REFLECTION

AUG 10 MONDAY

CARD OF THE DAY:

▷ INTENTION

▷ REFLECTION

AUG 11 TUESDAY

CARD OF THE DAY:

▷ INTENTION

▷ REFLECTION

AUG 12 WEDNESDAY

CARD OF THE DAY:

▷ INTENTION

▷ REFLECTION

AUG 13 THURSDAY

CARD OF THE DAY:

▷ INTENTION

▷ REFLECTION

AUG 14 FRIDAY

CARD OF THE DAY:

▷ INTENTION

▷ REFLECTION

AUG 15 SATURDAY   CARD OF THE DAY:

▷ INTENTION   ▷ REFLECTION

AUG 16 SUNDAY   CARD OF THE DAY:

▷ INTENTION   ▷ REFLECTION

AUG 17 MONDAY   CARD OF THE DAY:

▷ INTENTION   ▷ REFLECTION

AUG 18 TUESDAY   CARD OF THE DAY:

▷ INTENTION   ▷ REFLECTION

AUG 19 WEDNESDAY   CARD OF THE DAY:

▷ INTENTION   ▷ REFLECTION

AUG 20 THURSDAY   CARD OF THE DAY:

▷ INTENTION   ▷ REFLECTION

AUG 21 FRIDAY   CARD OF THE DAY:

▷ INTENTION   ▷ REFLECTION

AUG 22 SATURDAY   CARD OF THE DAY:

▷ INTENTION   ▷ REFLECTION

AUG 23 SUNDAY   CARD OF THE DAY:

▷ INTENTION   ▷ REFLECTION

AUG 24 MONDAY   CARD OF THE DAY:

▷ INTENTION   ▷ REFLECTION

AUG 25 TUESDAY   CARD OF THE DAY:

▷ INTENTION   ▷ REFLECTION

AUG 26 WEDNESDAY   CARD OF THE DAY:

▷ INTENTION   ▷ REFLECTION

AUG 27 THURSDAY   CARD OF THE DAY:

▷ INTENTION   ▷ REFLECTION

AUG 28 FRIDAY   CARD OF THE DAY:

▷ INTENTION   ▷ REFLECTION

AUG 29 SATURDAY

CARD OF THE DAY:

▷ INTENTION

▷ REFLECTION

AUG 30 SUNDAY

CARD OF THE DAY:

▷ INTENTION

▷ REFLECTION

AUG 31 MONDAY

CARD OF THE DAY:

▷ INTENTION

▷ REFLECTION

INSIGHTS

SEPTEMBER

TEMPERANCE

After a month of deep contemplation and self-reflection, September gives you the opportunity to bring more balance and harmony into your life. You are being invited to balance and ground your energy this month, and to allow the life force to flow through you without force or resistance. Don't allow the small stuff to get to you – maintain an even temperament and things will flow easily. You will also begin to integrate the different parts of yourself and harmonize your various passions, interests, and goals so that you can move forward with a sense of wholeness and completion.

 ### RITUAL: GROUNDING YOUR ENERGY

First, find the Temperance card in your Tarot deck and connect with its energy. Then, go to your favorite place in nature where there is water – a creek, river, lake or beach. Stand in the water and feel it flowing gently over your feet. Ground yourself through the sand, rocks or pebbles underneath. Then tilt your face to the sky and feel the warmth of the sun on your skin. Connect to the Universal energy and feel it flowing down through you, in perfect balance and harmony.

 ### CRYSTAL: AQUAMARINE

The word Aquamarine takes its roots from the Latin *aqua marinus*, meaning "water of the sea. It is a soothing, calming stone that will help you to better ebb and flow with the energies that surround you.

ASTROLOGICAL INFLUENCES

September 9: Mars retrograde begins. Action could be stalled for the next couple of months, despite your efforts or desires. Use this time to review and set a solid plan so you're ready to move when Mars turns direct.

September 12: Jupiter stations direct. The abundance and expansion you've been preparing and waiting for could start to manifest.

September 22: Libra season. Harmonious relationships and inner balance are key. Meditate on the Justice Tarot card.

September 29: Saturn stations direct. Tensions and restrictions start to lift as you move forward with a stronger sense of discipline and responsibility.

INSIGHTS

SEPTEMBER 2

FULL MOON
IN PISCES

A dreamy full moon in Pisces can intensify your connection to spirit and your intuition. Celebrate the manifestation of your imaginings and release any wishful thinking that isn't serving you now.

1. What dreams have come into my consciousness in the last 6 months?

2. How can I manifest my dream and bring it into being?

3. What hidden emotions are being illuminated right now?

4. What am I trying to "escape"?

5. What is my intuition trying to tell me?

6. What do I need to release in order to dream big?

INSIGHTS

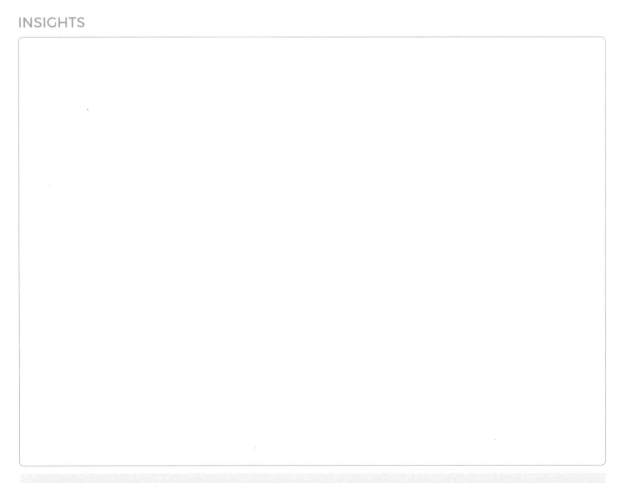

SEPTEMBER 17

NEW MOON IN VIRGO

The new moon in Virgo is an opportunity to get clear on how you want to be of service in the world and set your intentions around stepping into mastery. What will the peak version of you be focused on in this lunar cycle?

1. What needs my focus and attention right now?

2. How can I improve my career?

3. How can I improve my health?

4. How can I best serve at this time?

5. How can I bring a greater sense of order to my life?

6. What is my highest intention for my self-mastery?

INSIGHTS

SEP 01 TUESDAY

CARD OF THE DAY:

▷ INTENTION

▷ REFLECTION

SEP 02 WEDNESDAY

CARD OF THE DAY:

▷ INTENTION

▷ REFLECTION

SEP 03 THURSDAY

CARD OF THE DAY:

▷ INTENTION

▷ REFLECTION

SEP 04 FRIDAY

CARD OF THE DAY:

▷ INTENTION

▷ REFLECTION

SEP 05 SATURDAY

CARD OF THE DAY:

▷ INTENTION

▷ REFLECTION

SEP 06 SUNDAY

CARD OF THE DAY:

▷ INTENTION

▷ REFLECTION

SEP 07 MONDAY

CARD OF THE DAY:

▷ INTENTION

▷ REFLECTION

SEP 08   TUESDAY   CARD OF THE DAY:

▷ INTENTION   ▷ REFLECTION

SEP 09   WEDNESDAY   CARD OF THE DAY:

▷ INTENTION   ▷ REFLECTION

SEP 10   THURSDAY   CARD OF THE DAY:

▷ INTENTION   ▷ REFLECTION

SEP 11   FRIDAY   CARD OF THE DAY:

▷ INTENTION   ▷ REFLECTION

SEP 12   SATURDAY   CARD OF THE DAY:

▷ INTENTION   ▷ REFLECTION

SEP 13   SUNDAY   CARD OF THE DAY:

▷ INTENTION   ▷ REFLECTION

SEP 14   MONDAY   CARD OF THE DAY:

▷ INTENTION   ▷ REFLECTION

SEP 15 TUESDAY   CARD OF THE DAY:

▷ INTENTION   ▷ REFLECTION

SEP 16 WEDNESDAY   CARD OF THE DAY:

▷ INTENTION   ▷ REFLECTION

SEP 17 THURSDAY   CARD OF THE DAY:

▷ INTENTION   ▷ REFLECTION

SEP 18 FRIDAY   CARD OF THE DAY:

▷ INTENTION   ▷ REFLECTION

SEP 19 SATURDAY   CARD OF THE DAY:

▷ INTENTION   ▷ REFLECTION

SEP 20 SUNDAY   CARD OF THE DAY:

▷ INTENTION   ▷ REFLECTION

SEP 21 MONDAY   CARD OF THE DAY:

▷ INTENTION   ▷ REFLECTION

SEP 22 TUESDAY

CARD OF THE DAY:

▷ INTENTION

▷ REFLECTION

SEP 23 WEDNESDAY

CARD OF THE DAY:

▷ INTENTION

▷ REFLECTION

SEP 24 THURSDAY

CARD OF THE DAY:

▷ INTENTION

▷ REFLECTION

SEP 25 FRIDAY

CARD OF THE DAY:

▷ INTENTION

▷ REFLECTION

SEP 26 SATURDAY

CARD OF THE DAY:

▷ INTENTION

▷ REFLECTION

SEP 27 SUNDAY

CARD OF THE DAY:

▷ INTENTION

▷ REFLECTION

SEP 28 MONDAY

CARD OF THE DAY:

▷ INTENTION

▷ REFLECTION

SEP 29 TUESDAY   CARD OF THE DAY:

▷ INTENTION   ▷ REFLECTION

SEP 30 WEDNESDAY   CARD OF THE DAY:

▷ INTENTION   ▷ REFLECTION

INSIGHTS

FALL EQUINOX SPREAD

The Fall Equinox (September 23 in the Northern Hemisphere; March 20 in the Southern Hemisphere) is the time of harvest. After the abundance of the Summer, it is time to reap what you have sown, celebrate with deep appreciation, then bunker down for the Winter season.

This is the perfect time for slowing down, expressing gratitude for what you have achieved, and gathering your resources for the Winter period. Use the following Tarot spread around the time of the Fall Equinox to connect with this sacred energy.

1. What have I achieved during the Summer period?

2. What is the bounty of my harvest?

3. What am I truly grateful for?

4. What resources are available to me now?

5. What resources do I need to gather?

6. What can I release and let go?

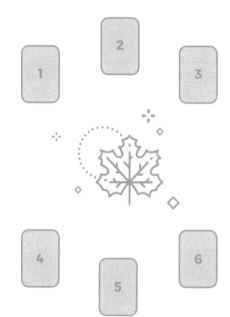

INSIGHTS

INSIGHTS

FALL EQUINOX INTENTIONS

Holding the energy and insight of your Fall Equinox Tarot Reading, set your intentions for the next three months:

OCTOBER

THE WORLD

In October, there is a sense of wholeness and completion as all of your triumphs and tribulations have come full circle and you can now sit in this beautiful place of being able to reflect on the past 12 months, honoring your achievements and tuning into your spiritual lessons. This is the perfect time to express gratitude for what you have created and harvested so far this year. It is also a good time to close out any projects and tie up any loose ends so that you are ready to embrace the new opportunities that are flowing your way.

 ### RITUAL: GRATITUDE AND CLOSURE

Take out the World card from your Tarot deck and place it in front of you, drawing in its energy. Light a candle and say out loud, "I open this sacred space and give thanks for all that I have experienced this year." Now, reflect on your achievements and experiences of the past 12 months and write them down in your journal. Don't just limit yourself to the successes – also reflect on the challenging moments of this year and the opportunities that emerged from those challenges. Now, reflect on what you have learned from the year and write these lessons down. Finally, reflect on how you can bring a sense of closure and completion to this cycle. To end the ritual, blow out the candle, saying out loud, "I close this sacred space and give thanks for all that I have experienced this year."

 ### CRYSTAL: AMETHYST

A high-vibrational and protective stone, Amethyst balances out the highs and lows of life, bringing peace and understanding. It helps you to remain focused and appreciative of all the blessings around you.

 ### ASTROLOGICAL INFLUENCES

October 4: Pluto stations direct. Just in time for the intensity of Scorpio season, Pluto moves forward, inviting you to embark on your transformational journey.

October 13: The last Mercury retrograde for the year begins in Scorpio (enters Libra October 27). You may feel called to reevaluate the power of your words.

October 22: Scorpio season begins. A time for deep transformation. Meditate on the Death Tarot card.

INSIGHTS

OCTOBER 1
FULL MOON IN ARIES

Honor your inner warrior with the Full Moon in Aries. Celebrate the ways you've grown into your strength and release the fears that hold you back.

1. What have I brought to life in the last 6 months?

2. Where do I need to show up with courage?

3. How can I release stress and tension from my body?

4. What does my inner warrior want me to know now?

5. Where do I need to be more selfish in my life?

6. What do I need to release in order to dare greatly?

INSIGHTS

We love seeing you use your Biddy Tarot Planner! Completed this spread? Make sure you post a pic on Instagram and be sure to use the hashtag **#biddytarotplanner** so we can celebrate with you!

104 | 2020 BIDDY TAROT PLANNER

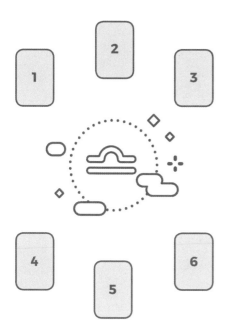

OCTOBER 16
NEW MOON IN LIBRA

A new moon in Libra is a beautiful time to explore your personal values and the environment and relationships that will support you to feel balanced.

1. Where can I bring more harmony to my life?

2. What can I do to balance my emotions?

3. How can I create more beauty in my environment?

4. What will help me feel at peace?

5. How can I form strong bonds with others?

6. What is my highest intention for my relationships?

INSIGHTS

OCTOBER 31
FULL MOON IN TAURUS

Taurus full moon brings the focus to your physical resources and sense of peace. Luxuriate in sensual pleasures and release anything that feels like drama.

1. What resources have I gathered in the last 6 months?

2. How can I bring more serenity to my days?

3. Where can I cultivate reverence in my life?

4. What gifts will physical grounding bring me?

5. How can I be more present in the moment?

6. What do I need to release in order to simplify my life?

INSIGHTS

We love seeing you use your Biddy Tarot Planner! Completed this spread? Make sure you post a pic on Instagram and be sure to use the hashtag **#biddytarotplanner** so we can celebrate with you!

OCT 01 THURSDAY

CARD OF THE DAY:

▷ INTENTION

▷ REFLECTION

OCT 02 FRIDAY

CARD OF THE DAY:

▷ INTENTION

▷ REFLECTION

OCT 03 SATURDAY

CARD OF THE DAY:

▷ INTENTION

▷ REFLECTION

OCT 04 SUNDAY

CARD OF THE DAY:

▷ INTENTION

▷ REFLECTION

OCT 05 MONDAY

CARD OF THE DAY:

▷ INTENTION

▷ REFLECTION

OCT 06 TUESDAY

CARD OF THE DAY:

▷ INTENTION

▷ REFLECTION

OCT 07 WEDNESDAY

CARD OF THE DAY:

▷ INTENTION

▷ REFLECTION

OCT 08 THURSDAY   CARD OF THE DAY:

▷ INTENTION   ▷ REFLECTION

OCT 09 FRIDAY   CARD OF THE DAY:

▷ INTENTION   ▷ REFLECTION

OCT 10 SATURDAY   CARD OF THE DAY:

▷ INTENTION   ▷ REFLECTION

OCT 11 SUNDAY   CARD OF THE DAY:

▷ INTENTION   ▷ REFLECTION

OCT 12 MONDAY   CARD OF THE DAY:

▷ INTENTION   ▷ REFLECTION

OCT 13 TUESDAY   CARD OF THE DAY:

▷ INTENTION   ▷ REFLECTION

OCT 14 WEDNESDAY   CARD OF THE DAY:

▷ INTENTION   ▷ REFLECTION

OCT 15 THURSDAY   CARD OF THE DAY:

▷ INTENTION   ▷ REFLECTION

OCT 16 FRIDAY   CARD OF THE DAY:

▷ INTENTION   ▷ REFLECTION

OCT 17 SATURDAY   CARD OF THE DAY:

▷ INTENTION   ▷ REFLECTION

OCT 18 SUNDAY   CARD OF THE DAY:

▷ INTENTION   ▷ REFLECTION

OCT 19 MONDAY   CARD OF THE DAY:

▷ INTENTION   ▷ REFLECTION

OCT 20 TUESDAY   CARD OF THE DAY:

▷ INTENTION   ▷ REFLECTION

OCT 21 WEDNESDAY   CARD OF THE DAY:

▷ INTENTION   ▷ REFLECTION

OCT 22 THURSDAY

CARD OF THE DAY:

▷ INTENTION

▷ REFLECTION

OCT 23 FRIDAY

CARD OF THE DAY:

▷ INTENTION

▷ REFLECTION

OCT 24 SATURDAY

CARD OF THE DAY:

▷ INTENTION

▷ REFLECTION

OCT 25 SUNDAY

CARD OF THE DAY:

▷ INTENTION

▷ REFLECTION

OCT 26 MONDAY

CARD OF THE DAY:

▷ INTENTION

▷ REFLECTION

OCT 27 TUESDAY

CARD OF THE DAY:

▷ INTENTION

▷ REFLECTION

OCT 28 WEDNESDAY

CARD OF THE DAY:

▷ INTENTION

▷ REFLECTION

OCT 29 THURSDAY · CARD OF THE DAY:

▷ INTENTION

▷ REFLECTION

OCT 30 FRIDAY · CARD OF THE DAY:

▷ INTENTION

▷ REFLECTION

OCT 31 SATURDAY · CARD OF THE DAY:

▷ INTENTION

▷ REFLECTION

INSIGHTS

NOVEMBER

DEATH

While October invited you to bring closure to a major cycle in your life, November invites you to experience the metaphorical 'death' of it so that a new one can begin. You are in that in-between space where the end has come, but the new beginning has not yet blossomed. For some, this ending can bring sadness, disappointment, and grief. For others, it may bring relief and a renewed sense of freedom. Feel into what this 'death' brings up for you emotionally. You are also being called to let go of that which no longer serves you so you can embrace those new beginnings with even greater conviction. Resistance may rise up, but remind yourself that with death, there is life, and with life, there is death. By letting go, what are you allowing to emerge and grow? What transformation can you create?

 ### RITUAL: DEATH AND REBIRTH

This is an intense ritual, perhaps too intense for some, but also very powerful — so please do this ritual mindfully. Take out the Death card and light a candle. Meditate on the concept of death and transformation. Then when you are ready, bring your attention inwards and connect with your inner source of energy. Imagine that today is the last day of your life. You are stripped of your past and your identity, and all that is left is your pure source energy. You may even imagine yourself dying, melting into the ground, fading away. Then, imagine yourself being reborn and recreated from that pure source of energy. Experience a sense of peace and deep truth as you step fully into this transformation. You are refreshed and revitalized. And when you are ready, come back into the room and journal your experience.

 ### CRYSTAL: CARNELIAN

Known to help instill acceptance of 'the cycle of life', Carnelian is useful in grounding you to present reality, helping to distinguish what no longer serves you by learning to trust yourself and your perceptions. This high energy stone stimulates courage and helps to overcome negative conditioning that has been learned over time.

 ### ASTROLOGICAL INFLUENCES

November 3: Mercury retrograde ends.

November 21: Sagittarius season begins. Enjoy the playful energies, but be cautious of taking it too far. Meditate on the Temperance Tarot card.

November 28: Neptune direct. Foggy thinking may start to clear as you move forward with your dreams.

INSIGHTS

NOVEMBER 15

NEW MOON IN SCORPIO

Following on from the Death and Rebirth Ritual, the new moon in Scorpio is the ideal time to make conscious decisions about your transformation. Set your intentions about who you're becoming.

1. How can I align my feelings and my actions?

2. What is truly important to me?

3. How can I healthily express my deep emotional desires?

4. How can I integrate my Shadow self into my being?

5. Where do I need to be honest with myself?

6. What is my highest intention for my soul's truth?

INSIGHTS

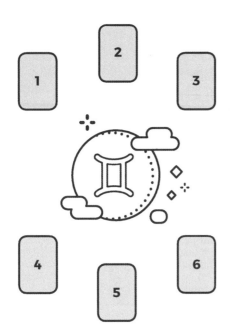

NOVEMBER 30
FULL MOON IN GEMINI

The full moon lunar eclipse in Gemini enhances your vitality and brings to light the ways you perceive the world. Release any feelings of boredom and explore your curiosities.

1. How have I heightened my perception in the last 6 months?

2. Where is my curiosity leading me?

3. How can I improve my physical and mental vitality?

4. How can I more fully witness the world?

5. Where do I need to introduce more variety into my life?

6. What do I need to release in order to communicate clearly?

INSIGHTS

NOV 01 SUNDAY   CARD OF THE DAY:

▷ INTENTION   ▷ REFLECTION

NOV 02 MONDAY   CARD OF THE DAY:

▷ INTENTION   ▷ REFLECTION

NOV 03 TUESDAY   CARD OF THE DAY:

▷ INTENTION   ▷ REFLECTION

NOV 04 WEDNESDAY   CARD OF THE DAY:

▷ INTENTION   ▷ REFLECTION

NOV 05 THURSDAY   CARD OF THE DAY:

▷ INTENTION   ▷ REFLECTION

NOV 06 FRIDAY   CARD OF THE DAY:

▷ INTENTION   ▷ REFLECTION

NOV 07 SATURDAY   CARD OF THE DAY:

▷ INTENTION   ▷ REFLECTION

NOV 08 SUNDAY

CARD OF THE DAY:

▷ INTENTION

▷ REFLECTION

NOV 09 MONDAY

CARD OF THE DAY:

▷ INTENTION

▷ REFLECTION

NOV 10 TUESDAY

CARD OF THE DAY:

▷ INTENTION

▷ REFLECTION

NOV 11 WEDNESDAY

CARD OF THE DAY:

▷ INTENTION

▷ REFLECTION

NOV 12 THURSDAY

CARD OF THE DAY:

▷ INTENTION

▷ REFLECTION

NOV 13 FRIDAY

CARD OF THE DAY:

▷ INTENTION

▷ REFLECTION

NOV 14 SATURDAY

CARD OF THE DAY:

▷ INTENTION

▷ REFLECTION

NOV 15 SUNDAY   CARD OF THE DAY:

▷ INTENTION   ▷ REFLECTION

NOV 16 MONDAY   CARD OF THE DAY:

▷ INTENTION   ▷ REFLECTION

NOV 17 TUESDAY   CARD OF THE DAY:

▷ INTENTION   ▷ REFLECTION

NOV 18 WEDNESDAY   CARD OF THE DAY:

▷ INTENTION   ▷ REFLECTION

NOV 19 THURSDAY   CARD OF THE DAY:

▷ INTENTION   ▷ REFLECTION

NOV 20 FRIDAY   CARD OF THE DAY:

▷ INTENTION   ▷ REFLECTION

NOV 21 SATURDAY   CARD OF THE DAY:

▷ INTENTION   ▷ REFLECTION

NOV 22 SUNDAY CARD OF THE DAY:

▷ INTENTION ▷ REFLECTION

NOV 23 MONDAY CARD OF THE DAY:

▷ INTENTION ▷ REFLECTION

NOV 24 TUESDAY CARD OF THE DAY:

▷ INTENTION ▷ REFLECTION

NOV 25 WEDNESDAY CARD OF THE DAY:

▷ INTENTION ▷ REFLECTION

NOV 26 THURSDAY CARD OF THE DAY:

▷ INTENTION ▷ REFLECTION

NOV 27 FRIDAY CARD OF THE DAY:

▷ INTENTION ▷ REFLECTION

NOV 28 SATURDAY CARD OF THE DAY:

▷ INTENTION ▷ REFLECTION

NOV 29 SUNDAY   CARD OF THE DAY:

▷ INTENTION   ▷ REFLECTION

NOV 30 MONDAY   CARD OF THE DAY:

▷ INTENTION   ▷ REFLECTION

INSIGHTS

DECEMBER

THE LOVERS

At the heart of it, the Lovers is about choice. Choice about who you spend time with. Choice about who you let into your life. Choice about how you interact with others and on what level. What are you choosing this month, especially when it comes to your relationships? Be mindful about your interactions with others and invest your energy with those who truly light you up or raise your vibration. And be open to exploring both the light and dark aspects of your relationships with others, taking the good with the bad and making conscious connections.

 ### RITUAL: OPENING THE HEART

Take out the Lovers card from your Tarot deck and reflect on its energy. Then, find a quiet place and light a candle and burn some rose or ylang ylang oil. Close your eyes and connect with your heart chakra. Visualize a ball of pink light radiating from your heart center. Feel this light growing and growing as it fills your body, then radiates out from you into your aura, your room, your neighborhood, and eventually into the world and Universe. Take a moment to feel this deep, radiant love. And say this affirmation 3 times: "I honor the love inside me and connect consciously with others." When you're ready, open your eyes and journal your experience.

 ### CRYSTAL: ROSE QUARTZ

The stone of peace and unconditional love. It is effective in drawing in those loving relationships and deflecting negative energies. Rose Quartz will help you open your heart to love and beauty by healing unexpressed heartaches and transmuting internalized pains that no longer serve you.

⊘ ASTROLOGICAL INFLUENCES

December 21: Jupiter conjunct Saturn in Aquarius (right at the tail end of Capricorn). Known as "the Great Conjunction", this rare transit only occurs every twenty years. This year, Jupiter and Saturn meet in the sky during the Solstice, intensifying the energies even further. A powerful end to the Year of the Emperor, this is a prime opportunity to expand, grow and create freedom within a stable structure.

INSIGHTS

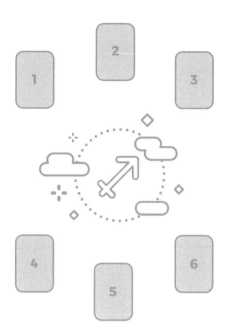

NEW MOON IN SAGITTARIUS

The new moon solar eclipse in Sagittarius encourages you to expand your awareness and perspective. Set intentions around adventures and experiences that will broaden your worldview.

1. What new experiences am I calling into my life?

2. Where do I need to expand my perspective and see things differently?

3. What new areas of learning can I explore?

4. How can I embrace adventure?

5. How can I nourish my faith?

6. What is my highest intention for my freedom?

INSIGHTS

DECEMBER 30

FULL MOON IN CANCER

Feel the feels with the new moon in Cancer, honoring the ways you have nurtured yourself and celebrating the divine feminine within. Release the barriers to your healing.

1. How have I nurtured my emotional self in the last 6 months?

2. Where in my life am I ready to heal?

3. How can I open my heart whilst maintaining healthy boundaries?

4. Which of my emotions are no longer serving my highest good?

5. What aspects of my Self need mothering now?

6. What do I need to release in order to trust life?

INSIGHTS

Don't forget to snap a pic of your reading and share on IG using the hashtag **#biddytarotplanner**. We love seeing you using your Biddy Tarot Planner in action and can't wait to celebrate with you!

DEC 01 TUESDAY

CARD OF THE DAY:

▷ INTENTION

▷ REFLECTION

DEC 02 WEDNESDAY

CARD OF THE DAY:

▷ INTENTION

▷ REFLECTION

DEC 03 THURSDAY

CARD OF THE DAY:

▷ INTENTION

▷ REFLECTION

DEC 04 FRIDAY

CARD OF THE DAY:

▷ INTENTION

▷ REFLECTION

DEC 05 SATURDAY

CARD OF THE DAY:

▷ INTENTION

▷ REFLECTION

DEC 06 SUNDAY

CARD OF THE DAY:

▷ INTENTION

▷ REFLECTION

DEC 07 MONDAY

CARD OF THE DAY:

▷ INTENTION

▷ REFLECTION

DEC 08   TUESDAY   CARD OF THE DAY:

▷ INTENTION   ▷ REFLECTION

DEC 09   WEDNESDAY   CARD OF THE DAY:

▷ INTENTION   ▷ REFLECTION

DEC 10   THURSDAY   CARD OF THE DAY:

▷ INTENTION   ▷ REFLECTION

DEC 11   FRIDAY   CARD OF THE DAY:

▷ INTENTION   ▷ REFLECTION

DEC 12   SATURDAY   CARD OF THE DAY:

▷ INTENTION   ▷ REFLECTION

DEC 13   SUNDAY   CARD OF THE DAY:

▷ INTENTION   ▷ REFLECTION

DEC 14   MONDAY   CARD OF THE DAY:

▷ INTENTION   ▷ REFLECTION

DEC 15 TUESDAY   CARD OF THE DAY:

▷ INTENTION   ▷ REFLECTION

DEC 16 WEDNESDAY   CARD OF THE DAY:

▷ INTENTION   ▷ REFLECTION

DEC 17 THURSDAY   CARD OF THE DAY:

▷ INTENTION   ▷ REFLECTION

DEC 18 FRIDAY   CARD OF THE DAY:

▷ INTENTION   ▷ REFLECTION

DEC 19 SATURDAY   CARD OF THE DAY:

▷ INTENTION   ▷ REFLECTION

DEC 20 SUNDAY   CARD OF THE DAY:

▷ INTENTION   ▷ REFLECTION

DEC 21 MONDAY   CARD OF THE DAY:

▷ INTENTION   ▷ REFLECTION

DEC 22 TUESDAY

CARD OF THE DAY:

▷ INTENTION

▷ REFLECTION

DEC 23 WEDNESDAY

CARD OF THE DAY:

▷ INTENTION

▷ REFLECTION

DEC 24 THURSDAY

CARD OF THE DAY:

▷ INTENTION

▷ REFLECTION

DEC 25 FRIDAY

CARD OF THE DAY:

▷ INTENTION

▷ REFLECTION

DEC 26 SATURDAY

CARD OF THE DAY:

▷ INTENTION

▷ REFLECTION

DEC 27 SUNDAY

CARD OF THE DAY:

▷ INTENTION

▷ REFLECTION

DEC 28 MONDAY

CARD OF THE DAY:

▷ INTENTION

▷ REFLECTION

DEC 29   TUESDAY

CARD OF THE DAY:

▷ INTENTION

▷ REFLECTION

DEC 30   WEDNESDAY

CARD OF THE DAY:

▷ INTENTION

▷ REFLECTION

DEC 31   THURSDAY

CARD OF THE DAY:

▷ INTENTION

▷ REFLECTION

INSIGHTS

WINTER SOLSTICE SPREAD

Winter Solstice (December 21 in the Northern Hemisphere; June 20 in the Southern Hemisphere), is the perfect time to go within, to step into the darkness and hibernate, and to reflect on your shadow self (the part of you that you try to deny or hide from others), before emerging once again into the light.

Use the following Tarot spread during the Winter Solstice to connect with this sacred energy.

1. What is the essence of my inner shadow self?

2. What can I learn from my shadow self?

3. How can I bring my shadow self into the light?

4. What lights me up from within?

5. What new seeds am I planting?

6. What do I need to release in order to create space for growth?

INSIGHTS

INSIGHTS

WINTER SOLSTICE INTENTIONS

Holding the energy and insight of your Winter Solstice Tarot Reading, set your intentions for the next three months:

2020 REFLECTION

As we come to the end of 2020, take some time to reflect on the past 12 months and prepare yourself for the year to come. Go back to the New Year's Tarot Spread you completed in January and reflect on what has emerged over the course of the year.

Then, go through the questions below and for each one, journal your intuitive thoughts first, then if you feel called to do so, draw a Tarot card to help you go deeper.

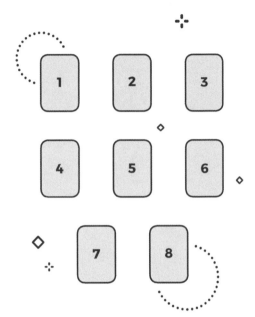

1. What were my biggest achievements for 2020?

2. What were my biggest challenges for 2020?

3. How have I developed as a person?

4. What did I learn in 2020?

5. How would I describe 2020 in just 3 words?

6. What is now complete?

7. What continues into 2021?

8. What new seeds and opportunities are being planted?

1. WHAT WERE MY BIGGEST ACHIEVEMENTS FOR 2020?

Don't forget to snap a pic of your reading and share on IG using the hashtag **#biddytarotplanner**. We love seeing you using your Biddy Tarot Planner in action and can't wait to celebrate with you!

2. WHAT WERE MY BIGGEST CHALLENGES FOR 2020?

3. HOW HAVE I DEVELOPED AS A PERSON?

4. WHAT DID I LEARN IN 2020?

5. HOW WOULD I DESCRIBE 2020 IN JUST 3 WORDS?

6. WHAT IS NOW COMPLETE?

7. WHAT CONTINUES INTO 2021?

8. WHAT NEW SEEDS AND OPPORTUNITIES ARE BEING PLANTED?

RESOURCES FOR YOUR TAROT JOURNEY

FREE PLANNER BONUSES

Go to www.biddytarot.com/planner-bonus and I'll give you FREE access to a ton of bonus resources to help you make the most of your Biddy Tarot Planner. These include:

- ⊙ Video tutorials on how to use the Planner
- ⊙ Full Moon & New Moon Rituals and Visualizations to maximize the power and potency of the lunar cycles
- ⊙ A guide to navigating Mercury Retrograde and a special Mercury Retrograde Tarot spread
- ⊙ Print-your-own Tarot cards to use inside of the Planner
- ⊙ Access to November & December from the 2019 Biddy Tarot Planner so you can get started straight away
- ⊙ And so much more!

Download (for free!) at www.biddytarot.com/planner-bonus.

THE ULTIMATE GUIDE TO TAROT CARD MEANINGS

The Ultimate Guide to Tarot Card Meanings has everything you need to read the Tarot cards as simply as reading a magazine. Just imagine: all the Tarot card meanings you could ever want, right at your fingertips in this comprehensive, 330+ page reference guide. You'll never need to buy another book on Tarot card meanings again!!

Available for purchase at www.biddytarot.com/guide.

Learn more about these resources — and our full range of Tarot courses and programs — to help you on your journey at www.biddytarot.com/shop.

EVERYDAY TAROT CARD DECK

The *Everyday Tarot* Card Deck offers a fresh approach to Tarot, with a modern, beautifully illustrated deck, a helpful guide to the cards, and a beautiful keepsake box.

Everyday Tarot brings a new perspective to the cards, giving modern soul-seekers the tools they need to access their inner wisdom and create an inspired life. This charming package, featuring stunning cards and a magnetic closure, will appeal to Tarot veterans and novices alike!

This kit includes:

- ⊙ A mini Tarot deck, with 78 fully-illustrated cards.
- ⊙ An 88-page mini book, with card meanings and sample spreads.

Available for purchase at www.everydaytarot.com/deck.

INTUITIVE TAROT

In this modern and practical guide, you'll go on an exciting, 31-day journey to understand the essence of the Tarot and tune into your inner wisdom, so that you can live life to your fullest potential (using the Tarot as your guide).

Intuitive Tarot breaks down the complex systems of the Tarot into bite-sized, actionable steps. Work your way through the daily activities and you'll be reading Tarot with ease - from Day One!

In this 31 day experience, you will:

- Learn to confidently read Tarot for yourself and others

- Discover a simple way to interpret any card quickly and accurately

- End the frustration of trying to memorize all 78 card meanings

- Unlock the secret to impactful and insightful readings

- Learn practical Tarot wisdom, from Brigit's 25-year journey as a professional Tarot reader and over 10,000 readings

- Practice what you learn every day and ultimately become a better Tarot reader

- Start to trust your intuition and lead the life you're meant to live – your way

Available for purchase at www.biddytarot.com/tarot-guides/intuitive-tarot

EVERYDAY TAROT

Manifest the Life You Want with Tarot as Your Guide

Everyday Tarot takes a fresh approach to a timeless art, empowering modern soul-seekers with the confidence and skills to access inner wisdom and create an inspired life. Approach the cards with an open heart as you master Tarot basics and learn to draw on your own intuition to fulfil your deepest desires and wildest dreams.

Infused with the knowledge and personal experiences of Brigit Esselmont, founder of the popular and authoritative Biddy Tarot, this contemporary spin on the cards is uplifting, powerful, and practical.

Whether you're contemplating a job change, searching for your higher purpose, or looking for romantic guidance, Everyday Tarot is filled with clear questions and insightful card spreads that will help you divine your true path.

With actionable tips, soulful activities, and everyday rituals, novices and veterans alike will learn to view Tarot as an invitation to look within as they set and achieve goals, make important decisions, and achieve clarity in their daily lives.

Learn more at www.everydaytarot.com.

Made in the USA
San Bernardino, CA
04 December 2019

60820997R00075